Praise for *The Es̶p̶ ̶.̶.̶.̶u̶i̶i̶o̶n̶ Playbook*

As someone who has played and coached football professionally, I can tell you that the collegiate esports athletes I currently coach require the same training and dedication as those in traditional sports. In this book, Chris, Steve, Christine, and Jesse highlight the benefits of esports programs in schools and show how esports is changing the game in how we perceive what is a sport and who is an athlete. This is required reading for anyone interested in how to create a successful esports program that provides opportunities for all students to be a part of a team.

—**Ahman Green**, four-time Pro Bowl running back, Green Bay Packers, head coach of esports, Lakeland University

Hands down, the best guide to scholastic esports ever written! In this book, thought leaders in gaming and education have assembled an unparalleled array of data, strategies, tools, tips, and tricks to enable any school, community organization, or group to start and grow successful STEM-based hands-on scholastic esports organizations. Newbies, novices, and know-it-alls can use it to build custom gaming programs for kids in lower, middle, and high school.

—**Laylah Bulman**, senior program officer, Samueli Foundation, founder, Florida Scholastic Esports League

In esports, the players are the experts in the game, while the coaches are the experts in communication, planning, coordination, and attitude. Too many coaches and directors misunderstand what it is all about. Christine, Steve, Chris, and Jesse have perfectly captured the "why" of esports. If you want to create a program that enriches the lives of your players and community, THIS is the book. If you're only in esports to win, you never will until you understand how to give guidance, celebrate the little victories, provide support in troubling times, and (of course) teach—and this is STILL the book.

—**Dr. Chris "Doc" Haskell**, head coach, Boise State University, 2020 Collegiate Esports Coach of the Year (NAECAD), and 2020 Director of the Year (NACE)

Esports in education is not a fad—it allows us to facilitate new opportunities for our students. Traditional sports have been seen as a way for students to collaborate, communicate, and lead. In *The Esports Education Playbook*, authors who truly know the ecosystem lay out why your student or school should take this fast-growing collaborative sport seriously. This is not your father's Atari—this is the future!

—**Don Wettrick**, president, STARTedUP Foundation,
author of *Pure Genius*

As we start a statewide esports push in Washington, the information in this book has been vital in covering every aspect of that process. *The Esports Education Playbook* has been informative and exciting as we begin this endeavor. It is a must-read for anyone interested in moving the needle on esports in the school, district, region, or state.

—**Tammie Schrader**, regional science coordinator and computer science coordinator, Educational Service District 101, Northeast Washington LASER director

The Esports Education Playbook is at once a guide, an inspiration, and a call to action. Kids looking to start a league, teachers hoping for guidance, and school leaders needing a reason to provide access to esports clubs will all find this book to be an amazing resource. It's also a must-read for educators like me who don't self-identify as "gamers" but want to better understand and support the esports community.

—**Becky Keene**, educator, speaker, and author
of *Sail the 7 Cs with Microsoft Education*

From start to finish, *The Esports Education Playbook* provides an excellent foundation for anyone interested in starting an esports team. Chris, Steve, Christine, and Jesse share so many great resources that can help a novice educator or expert educator start, sustain, and grow a successful esports program that provides opportunities for all students to participate and be part of a team.

—**Alfonso Mendoza Jr., MEd,** host of the *My EdTech Life!* podcast

This is a beautiful compilation of the knowledge, insight, and wisdom gained from an innovative community of educators integrating esports into our programs. Wherever you may be in your journey of exploring scholastic esports, this book will take you beyond the pages of information into the stories of educators who are pioneering the work of integrating learning and intentional play.

—**Jorel Battac**, esports scholastic instructional coach, Orange County Department of Education

The Esports Education Playbook is a comprehensive look at why games are so vitally important to learning. The authors all possess evident expertise in the subject, and they dive beyond the buzzwords and deep into discussions of implementation and what incorporating games into the classroom can do for students both cognitively and emotionally. This book is a true must-read for anyone looking to level up and bring esports to their school or classroom, as it provides the what, the why, and a practical look at the how of esports.

—**Adam Bellow**, cofounder, Breakout EDU

Esports has been lurking on the fringe for many years, but recently, it has exploded into a multibillion-dollar enterprise that spans the globe. This amazing book explains how any educator can help students engage in esports. By dismantling myths associated with gaming, *The Esports Education Playbook* addresses the Bowser in the room and answers all of the questions an educator might have. As an avid gamer myself, I am excited to see a well-written book that explains the value of esports to the larger educational community. It's worth hitting pause and setting your controller down to read this book to help bring esports to your educational community.

—**Nicholas Provenzano**, teacher and author of *Your Starter Guide to Makerspaces*

Scholastic esports is a terrific informal learning opportunity for kids—particularly those who have never been on a team before, much less coached one. *The Esports Education Playbook* is the right book at the right time. Packed with useful tips and information from scholastic esports practitioners and supported by the latest in character education and social and emotional learning research, this book should be required reading for all stakeholders. Game on!

—**Matthew Farber, Ed.D.**, assistant professor of technology, innovation, and pedagogy, University of Northern Colorado

Esports extends the opportunity for students to be more involved at school. *The Esports Education Playbook* opens the door for any school or organization that is looking to provide students with the opportunity to engage in esports. From concise how-to steps for developing a program to the more abstract aspects of how esports promotes SEL, this book helps readers to make meaningful connections across all aspects of school life. It's a must-read for any coach, educator, parent, or academic leader who is looking to bring the latest and greatest of opportunities to students.

—**Alice Keeler**, teacher, edtech expert, Google innovator

The Esports Education Playbook is a great template for instructors trying to understand the explosion of esports and its greater impact within the education system. The authors' deliberate approach makes it a great resource for anyone looking into how esports can transform extracurricular programs across a school or district. This isn't about students playing games; it's about inclusion and a real approach to engaging students.

—**Blake Everhart**, customer solutions manager, ViewSonic

The Esports Education Playbook is a fantastic entry point to the fast-growing world of scholastic esports. But more than simply laying out background information and guidance on how educators can implement a program in their school, Chris, Steve, Christine, and Jesse provide a clear and direct vision for how esports promotes equitable opportunities for diverse student populations. If you are looking to ensure that all of your students are provided access and opportunity in ways that extend beyond traditional school offerings, there is no better place to start than here.

—**Kenneth Shelton**, educational strategist,
equity and inclusion consultant

The Esports Education Playbook is an all-encompassing guide on intentional esports opportunities in K–12 education. Christine, Steve, Jesse, and Chris craftily illustrate how, by going beyond video games, impactful esports programs can equip students to be empathetic, resilient, and ambitious game-changers. A must-read for all!

—**Samantha Anton**, chief operating officer,
North America Scholastic Esports Federation

Whether you are just getting started with esports or have developed a program already, *The Esports Education Playbook* offers a unique opportunity to learn from the experiences of leaders in the field. This book includes detailed steps on how to start an esports program as well as creative advice to improve an existing program. It also shares meaningful information regarding the impact esports will have on your students and their larger communities. From getting the capital you need to executing a successful plan, *The Esports Education Playbook* is an invaluable resource you don't want to miss.

—**Anna Hanson**, sales director, ByteSpeed

The Esports Education Playbook is a comprehensive guide to all facets of considering, evaluating, starting, and sustaining an esports program. Chris, Steve, Christine, and Jesse have created a guide that provides a fundamental grounding in how and why esports should be considered part of your school community. There's even a history lesson that shows that the esports community has existed for years. This is the starting point for making sure esports becomes a part of the educational landscape.

—**Alex J. Podchaski**, director of educational and information technology, North Broward Preparatory School

Finally! *The Esports Education Playbook* walks any hopeful teacher or administrator through the esports movement that is spreading like wildfire! This book has all the answers (even to questions you wouldn't know to ask) for embarking on a fantastic esports journey. *The Esports Education Playbook* takes the reader through the history of gaming and esports development in a fun narrative. It then launches a practical, step-by-step guide that explains how esports can be harnessed for any school or district. Now that the impact of COVID-19 is redefining education and sports, this book couldn't be timelier.

—**Jennifer Cronk**, director of technology, Newburgh Enlarged City School District

With over 90 percent of youth playing video games, gaming has become the new literacy for an upcoming generation, and esports the outlet by which they challenge, socialize, educate, and entertain themselves. From early pioneers in education esports, *The Esports*

Education Playbook offers readers a map for navigating digital culture and game-centered learning. Grounded in social and emotional perspectives on how students thrive as humans, the authors shine a light on the importance of health and wellness. They change perceptions about esports around longstanding issues of gameplay, such as gender inequality, screen time, violence, and toxic gaming culture, and provide educators with insightful tips on working with stakeholders. The book also offers a clear roadmap for designing and managing a transformative esports program in schools.

—**Dr. Lisa Dawley**, executive director, Jacobs Institute for Innovation in Education at the University of San Diego

The Esports Education Playbook is poised to transform the student experience. Esports is so much more than just playing a video game; it is an opportunity for you to enhance communication and grow leaders while giving each student a chance to play and build relationships with their peers. Let this book serve as a guide for those of you looking to create a school-to-career pipeline or simply create an extracurricular program. It is packed with great ideas on how to get started.

—**Jim Sill**, founder and head coach, Deploy Learning

The authors of this book guide us through the meaningful adoption of esports as a catalyst for positive change in education. As a teacher, coach, and ski school director, I have experienced the positive impact team sports have on young adults' ability to collaborate with a sense of common purpose toward both athletic and work-related goals. I have also been the source of tears, heartbreak, and anger when I've had to communicate that there simply were not enough team jerseys to give out in order to give every student the opportunity to participate in traditional school athletics. The promise of esports is increased access to meaningful, team-based experiences and growth opportunities for our students. This pragmatic guide effectively helps us to both conceptualize and implement esports in schools.

—**Dr. Micah Shippee**, chief executive officer, Ready Learner One

These four educators have put their extensive and impressive careers on public display, declaring in unashamed and proud voices that their shared passion for scholastic esports is not the fad of the moment or a COVID-fueled money grab but an actual, life-changing response to tired, discriminatory, and, frankly, useless classroom practices that have not done anything but marginalize and stereotype some students. This easy to read, not-too-technical playbook covers everything a school administrator, community-based organization, or inquisitive parent needs to know about esports. You'll be amazed at what you and your students can achieve.

—**Kevin Brown**, esports program specialist, curriculum developer, and teacher, Orange County Department of Education and NASEF

The Esports Playbook offers key strategies that you don't want to miss. The playbook is the first of its kind and will definitely reshape how educators see esports in education. The playbook provides a long-needed rallying cry for other educators to break into a market that was previously frowned upon. Education must be reshaped to accommodate the many soft skills that are needed in 2020, and this book gives you the tools that are necessary to do that.

—**Kimberly Lane Clark**, director of blended learning

Wouldn't it be great if there was a way to integrate student passions outside of the classroom into the school experience? If you are that educator who loses sleep over your disconnected students, then *The Esports Education Playbook* is a must-read. With actionable advice on developing an esports program, the book not only serves as your own personal trainer, but also proactively addresses some of the stereotypes associated with esports. Crafted so that even the most novice gamer can follow along, this book contains everything an educator needs to unleash the learning for any student.

—**Jeffery Heil**, classroom teacher and edtech consultant

Showing that esports is so much more than just playing a video game, *The Esports Education Playbook* does a phenomenal job of addressing the social and emotional learning that is aligned with school esports programs. By providing every student an opportunity to be recognized and celebrated, *The Esports Education Playbook* paints a picture for how your school culture and community can be transformed.

—**Wiley Brazier V**, leadership and technology integration consultant, change agent

Full of hopeful, helpful, hands-on examples, *The Esports Education Playbook* is a must-read for anyone interested in learning how to leverage the power of games to transform the student experience. Chris, Steve, Christine, and Jesse understand the risks, challenges, and opportunities associated with launching esports programs in schools and community-based settings, and they offer guidance full of wisdom and practical know-how. They show us the importance of connecting with a broad range of stakeholders, including students, to create a custom program for any school or community looking to engage youth in an esports experience.

—**Katie Salen Tekinbaş**, professor, department of informatics, University of California, Irvine

The Esports Education Playbook takes a fascinating and comprehensive look at esports in education. Esports have the potential to truly transform your school and give new opportunities for social and emotional learning to some of the children who need it most, and this guide takes you step-by-step through the process of understanding and implementing them in your own organization. Whether you're new to esports or a seasoned pro, the stories and examples in this book are sure to inspire and resonate with you.

—**Faye Nicole Ellis**, director of digital technology, Thomas's School, Clapham

If you are interested in esports but unsure where to begin, *The Esports Education Playbook* is for you. Christine, Jesse, Steve, and Chris have outlined everything you need to know. This book guides the reader in implementing a robust esports program to transform school culture. Esports is much more than simply playing games, and you need this book to ensure you are well equipped to plan a successful program.

—**Knikole Taylor**, learner, trainer, speaker

For a classroom teacher like me who is looking to get an esports program off the ground, this book provides the proper framework, guidance, and rationale to get a program started! You will not be disappointed!

—**Donnie Piercey**, fifth grade teacher

The Esports Education Playbook is the definitive guide for implementing purposeful esports programs in secondary eduction. Written from an approachable but deeply researched perspective, this guidebook for esports discusses the what, how, and why of creating meaningful esports in schools. The authors dive straight into the misconceptions of gaming and tackle important questions about how esports actually cultivates the social and emotional well-being of students while also providing avenues for funding that simply did not exist years ago. The authors also manage to tackle the logistics of implementing esports in schools while also meeting the needs of a diverse group of learners—something that is sorely needed in every conversation about education. This text will help you meet the potential of esports in your school head on through the design, development, and implementation process with the perspectives of the best experts we have in this space.

—Lindsay Portnoy, PhD, cognitive scientist, researcher, and educator

The Esports Education Playbook is one of the first books to guide educators and advocates through the ins and outs of implementing a successful esports program. From the step-by-step process of organizing and funding a program to the social and emotional benefits it can bring to the learning community, readers can trust that the authors are leaving no challenge unaddressed, as this book serves as the ultimate guide!

—Jessica Williams, technology integration specialist

The Esports Education Playbook

— A READY LEARNER ONE BOOK —

THE
ESPORTS EDUCATION
PLAYBOOK

EMPOWERING EVERY LEARNER THROUGH INCLUSIVE GAMING

CHRIS   STEVE   CHRISTINE   JESSE
AVILES   ISAACS   LION-BAILEY   LUBINSKY

The Esports Education Playbook: Empowering Every Learner through Inclusive Gaming

© 2020 Chris Aviles, Steve Isaacs, Christine Lion-Bailey, and Jesse Lubinsky

This book is available at special discounts when purchased in quantity for educational purposes or for use as premiums, promotions, or fundraisers. For inquiries and details, contact the publisher at books@daveburgessconsulting.com.

Published by Dave Burgess Consulting, Inc.
San Diego, CA
DaveBurgessConsulting.com

Library of Congress Control Number: 2020944734
Paperback ISBN: 978-1-951600-50-1
Ebook ISBN: 978-1-951600-51-8

Cover and interior design by Liz Schreiter
Editing and production by Reading List Editorial:
readinglisteditorial.com

For my wife, Rachel. For my son,
Oliver: the world is yours.

CHRIS

To my mom and dad, who supported their geeky little
kid who spent hours in front of his Apple II+ computer
and Atari 2600. To Cathy, Grace, and Leila who
(mostly) support my love of pizza and video games.

STEVE

To Lilia and Jack: always take a chance on where
your heart leads you—it is there that you will find your
victory. To Mike, for being my teammate for life. To my
parents and sister, who endured many rounds of *Duck
Hunt*. To my coaches, who taught me the value of the
team before the importance of the game.

CHRISTINE

To Henry, for giving me that gold *Legend of Zelda*
cartridge and starting me down the path. To Billy, for
the Game Boy and the worlds it helped me travel. To
Sindee, for forgiving me for waking her up at 2:00 a.m.
to tell her I made it over the bridge in *Golden Axe*. To
the J-Squad (Jessica, Jordan, Jackson, and Josie),
and my mom, Lee, for their never-ending
love and support.

JESSE

CONTENTS

Foreword by James O'Hagan xix

Out of the Past 1

CHAPTER ONE   25

The Why of Esports in Schools

CHAPTER TWO   53

Changing Perceptions about Esports

CHAPTER THREE   71

Working with Stakeholders

CHAPTER FOUR   88

Designing an Esports Program

CONCLUSION   124

Looking to the Future

Appendix: An Esports Partner for K–12 Education 136

Glossary of Common Esports Terms 143

Notes 148

Acknowledgments 159

About the Authors. 161

More Books from Ready Learner One LLC 164

More from Dave Burgess Consulting, Inc.. 165

JAMES O'HAGAN

DIRECTOR, DIGITAL AND VIRTUAL LEARNING,
RACINE UNIFIED SCHOOL DISTRICT

FOUNDER AND PODCAST HOST,
THE ACADEMY OF ESPORTS

The idea of playing video games in school is nothing new. For as long as I was a student and have been an educator, video games have been a part of school culture. As a child, I caught *"Pac-Man* fever," and I played games like *Pitfall!*, *Galaga*, and *Street Fighter II*. Even when I started a computer club in my first year as an educator, it quickly became more of a video game club, in which we learned how to build computer networks, perform component upgrades, and, for some students, first surf the internet. For some of my students, it became a popular and safe social space to just hang out and play.

Fast-forward several years. While most schools have not, to date, embraced video games, video game culture is present in the classroom. Most recently, the *Fortnite* dance craze may have, at first, been a sociological oddity to some teachers. Students routinely broke out into Orange Justice, the Turk, or the Floss. Perhaps still oddly to some educators, this quickly became a normal part of youth culture.

Only recently, though, have schools begun to embrace video games, and particularly esports—in part because we have a population of educators and administrators who have grown up playing video games (myself, included). And when educators bring up video games to students, the typical response is first some hesitation, and then an infectious, almost irrepressible excitement. Many educators and students already share a common language around video games, but they rarely speak that language to each other. Esports is a fantastic vehicle with which to harness this shared excitement.

Unlike simply playing video games, participating in esports provides an organized and competitive experience based around a few select video games. It involves purposeful practice and a higher expectation of quality of experience. For students already possessing a sense of their own autonomy and competence, esports can help develop creativity, persistence, and performance (a classic example of self-determination theory).

Some educators get really excited about the idea of having an esports team at their school and engaging with their students in intrinsically motivating ways. They rush to implement a team by focusing first on what computers to buy and then on what games to play. Much like the way many one-to-one laptop programs were quickly implemented with the idea that "all the kids need is access to the technology, and learning will follow," resulting in disappointing outcomes, a similar mindset with an esports program can also be disappointing. Unfortunately, this has been a common mistake in the rush to implement esports in schools.

It is no longer cutting edge to have an esports team at your school. What is cutting edge is what you do with it.

Having been involved in scholastic esports since 2014, I have been a part of its rapid rise. A few short years ago, to have more than ten people in a room for a conference breakout session about the importance of bringing esports into schools—or even simply having esports included among the conference sessions—felt like a major victory. Now the topic of esports has become a darling of education and library conferences. It even has conferences of its own, like the UCI Esports Conference at the University of California, Irvine, and the National Association of Esports Coaches and Directors Academic Esports Conference & Expo.

Esports has rightfully garnered the attention of educators because it carries with it a motivating experience for children when properly implemented in schools. For educators stepping out of their comfort zones to entertain the idea of "playing video games in school," this book is a great resource from respected scholars with a relatively long-established involvement on this subject. Esports should never be a single turnkey solution sold by vendors but instead a custom experience based on the educational objectives of your school that includes student voice and choice. This book will help educators begin formulating their school's or district's purposeful first steps into esports.

Esports is much more than merely playing video games: it is a competitive and organized experience using video games as the core of a broad and rich ecosystem. This is an opportunity for us to redefine athletic culture in our schools, and to diversify participation in school activities for all children. Through esports, we can have meaningful conversations with our students around digital citizenship, exercise, nutrition, and wellness. We can help hard-to-reach students develop positive adult relationships around a common interest in esports, which can impact college and career potential.

Most importantly, esports allows us to meet our students where they are playing and competing and find a vital new avenue to honor the importance of play.

OUT OF THE PAST

To say esports is booming would be an understatement. In fact, esports made a huge splash in the news in the summer of 2019, when a sixteen-year-old teenager named Kyle Giersdorf, who goes by the online name "Bugha," won $3 million at the inaugural *Fortnite* World Cup, held at the USTA Billie Jean King National Tennis Center in New York.[1] That kind of money being won by such a young gamer was bound to draw attention from the masses. But this was just one moment that cast a light on an industry that has grown exponentially around the world.

The world of professional esports has exploded over the last few years and is expected to reach nearly $5 billion in value and a global audience of nearly six hundred million people in the year 2020.

More than two hundred million people watched the *League of Legends* World Championship in 2018—that's more than watched game seven of the World Series (23.5 million), the NBA championship game (20.4 million), and the Super Bowl (103.4 million).[2] The trend continued in 2019. The *League of Legends* World Championship finals—held in South Korea and hosted by the game's publisher, Riot Games—attracted almost one hundred million unique viewers online.[3] In comparison, the 2019 Super Bowl had just over ninety-eight million viewers, the smallest viewership number for the event since 2008.[4] In fact, many project that esports will be the second most watched sport in America, after football, by 2020.[5] In short, esports is not just a trend—the reality is that esports is a global sport.

The success of esports is not solely due to the viewership it draws, but also the investment that is going into growing the sport. In 2019 *Fortnite* announced a $100 million dollar investment (about two weeks of revenue) into their esports scene as the company brought competitive *Fortnite* to their 125 million players.[6] Because of investments like this by game developers, the professional esports scene has never had more players, events, or prize money.

Esports has passed the tipping point. It is here to stay, and educators should not only care, but should be excited. Thanks to the passion of students and the support of the video game industry, esports has begun to find a home in higher education. With thousands of the nation's colleges supporting esports at the club level and over 130 varsity-level programs, more than $9 million in esports scholarships are available for talented gamers. In 2019, the Big Ten Network (BTN) launched its first *League of Legends* competition on the ESL Collegiate platform. All fourteen of the Big Ten schools competed in the BTN *League of Legends* season.[7] Colleges are offering full-ride scholarships for esports games like *Overwatch, Counter-Strike: Global Offensive* (CS: GO), and others. The popularity of and opportunities in esports in higher education will only continue to grow by leaps and bounds.

To the delight of some and dismay of others, the growth of esports at the college level is leading to the growth of esports at the high school and middle school levels as the school-to-college esports pipeline develops.

With traditional sports, families, teachers, and coaches will do everything they can to help gifted athletes earn athletic scholarships. The efforts being poured into helping traditional athletes find a home at the collegiate level raises the question of what should be done in middle and high schools to help esports students find success at the collegiate level. We believe the time has come for K–12 schools to build an esports pipeline to successfully support aspiring esports athletes.

HOW DID WE GET HERE?

Before looking ahead, it's always important to look back at how we got to where we are. To help with that, we brought in our resident esports historian, Mike Washburn, to give us some insight into how esports evolved from simple gaming into an entire industry. Take it away, Mike!

There's a lot to say about the history of competitive gaming, or esports for short, and honestly, someone could write a whole book just about that. My friends Chris, Steve, Christine, and Jesse want this book to be about how educators can design and implement esports programs at the middle and high school levels, but with that context in mind, it still is worthwhile to take just a quick trip down memory lane. As with many great ideas, esports started with some smart folks trying to kill some time and stumbling onto a phenomenon. It's a great story.

The first competitive gaming event is widely considered to be Stanford University's *Spacewar!* event in 1972.[8] The *Spacewar!* craze among local university students was surprising at the time. It started with a few people playing and grew as others watched and eventually joined in. As things tend to do, it got competitive. That first event, called the Intergalactic *Spacewar!* Olympics, saw about two dozen players compete to be crowned the tournament's champion. The eventual winner, Bruce Baumgart, was a Stanford PhD student who went on to become a pioneer in digital archiving.

While *Spacewar!* was not a smash-hit video game, the next game was. *Space Invaders* burst on the scene in 1978 as the first "fixed shooter," defining a genre and amplifying the potential of stand-up arcade games as a form of entertainment. When *Space Invaders* was ported to the Atari 2600, sales of the console quadrupled. The *Space Invaders* championship had ten thousand participants, making it the biggest tournament ever hosted at the time.[9] The game industry and competitive gaming truly made a mark thanks to *Space Invaders*.

Games like *Donkey Kong* and *Pac-Man* shifted the notion that games were all about shooting. These games brought iconic characters onto the scene. *Donkey Kong* didn't just bring competitive gaming to the forefront: it brought video games in general into the spotlight. *Donkey Kong* is incredibly influential and one of the most iconic games in history. It was the birthplace of Mario, and what made Nintendo, Nintendo. *Donkey Kong* moved the focus away from the idea that video games were about shooting aliens or other characters, introducing the potential to incorporate action and strategy in a whole new way. There's also little doubt that *Donkey Kong*—how it was made and its gameplay mechanics—was the perfect vessel for early competitive gameplay.

Donkey Kong also introduced the world to one of esports's most controversial personalities: Billy Mitchell. The two are practically synonymous—you can't talk about *Donkey Kong* without talking about Billy Mitchell, and you can't talk about Billy Mitchell without talking about *Donkey Kong*. Whether the world of competitive gaming likes it or not (and there is a LOT to not like about Billy Mitchell), he just might be the most influential person in esports's young history. Let me explain.

Billy Mitchell gave competitive video gaming the personality it needed, making gamers themselves part of the growing narrative of video games. In 1982, he set a world record of 874,300 points in *Donkey Kong*.[10] News of his high score gave the popularity of the game a big boost. *Donkey Kong* was taking the world by storm, and Nintendo capitalized on every opportunity it could to showcase its landmark game and the game's iconic lead character, Jumpman, whom we would later know as Mario. Mitchell's high score was exactly what Nintendo needed, and his record went uncontested for almost twenty years. It even inspired a documentary, *The King of Kong: A Fistful of Quarters*, about classroom teacher Steve Wiebe trying to break that record.[11] Mitchell also held records in other games, including *Pac-Man*, *Ms. Pac-Man*, *BurgerTime*, and *Donkey Kong Jr.*, earning him the title of Video Game Player of the Century at the 1999 Tokyo Game Show.[12]

CUT SCENE

THE MOVIE THAT PREDICTED ESPORTS

While it's clear that there were many pivotal moments in the rise of esports to mainstream consciousness, one event in particular propelled it into popular culture. The 1989 movie *The Wizard*, starring Fred Savage and Christian Slater, served as a vehicle to promote video gaming, especially Nintendo products. The plot centered around a pair of young brothers traveling across the country to participate in a video game competition. At this time, tournaments (many of which mirror esports competitions) did not yet exist. Interestingly, this movie would never have been made had it not been for a shortage of the memory chips needed to make Nintendo cartridges.[13] One year after the movie was released, Nintendo launched the Nintendo World Championships, a gaming competition across the country that featured many prizes. One of this book's coauthors, Jesse Lubinsky, was thirteen at the time and competed in the tournament, playing *Super Mario Bros. 3*, the game at the center of the movie's plot. In a twist that paralleled the plot of the film, Jesse's young career in esports came to a screeching halt when an eight-year-old gamer thumped him in the first round. Who says life doesn't imitate art?

Video gaming became solidly embedded in popular culture in the 80s and 90s, the era of the Nintendo Entertainment System, Super Nintendo, and Sega Genesis. It was the time of *Final Fantasy, Street Fighter*, and *Super Mario*, and it represented the start of today's console wars. The rise of consoles brought us from a time when a gaming console in the home was a novelty to a time when it seemed like everyone you knew had one. The popularity of gaming consoles continued exploding in the early 2000s, when the Xbox and PlayStation entered the scene.

The growth of the game industry has also meant huge growth in competitive gaming. Esports is really nothing new—it's been huge in Korea since the 90s.

> That is when the government decided to build a national broadband network. This proliferation of high-speed internet allowed millions of young Koreans to play computer games with each other. And that happened at a time when such a thing was not widely possible elsewhere in the world.
>
> This happened due to the spread of PC angs, which are internet cafes. Millions of Koreans still go to a PC bang today to play games for hours, and many will be online games. With millions of people playing with and against each other, it was only a matter of time that it became a competitive esport.[14]

This was also an interesting time for competitive gaming. We saw glimpses of what the future might look like and its potential appeal. For example, the game *Street Fighter*. By the turn of the century it had become not just a popular video game, but a popular competitive game, with tournaments taking place all over the world and its best players becoming known figures in the space. While the matchup "Daigo versus Justin" might not mean much to the average reader, to many gamers it holds as much weight as Magic Johnson versus Larry Bird does to classic NBA fans. These two gamers produced what many consider an iconic moment in esports history at the semifinals of the 2004 Evolution Championship Series (better known simply as "Evo 2004").[15]

At this point Evo had already been around for six years and had established itself as one of the most popular tournaments in the world. The two players, Daigo Umehara and Justin Wong, were regarded as best in the world. They had never actually played against each other, yet they had already established a rivalry due to their different opinions on the most effective methods to play the game. Their meeting was eagerly anticipated, to put it mildly. With Daigo playing as Ken and Justin as Chun-Li, each had won one round. The final round started off poorly for Daigo, and Justin was preparing to finish him off with Chun-Li's special move, the "Houyokusen" After he successfully activated the move, things got crazy. To everyone's amazement, Daigo began to parry every single attack in the move. The parries to Chun-Li's flurry of kicks seemed practically supernatural. In any other match this would have been the end, but as the successive parries continued, the crowd realized what was happening and reacted explosively. To top it off, after Chun-Li's special had concluded, Daigo executed his own special attack and was able to finish Justin off. Now referred to as "Evo Moment 37," this famous face-off is immortalized on YouTube here: http://bit.ly/evo37. Watch the video and you'll immediately understand why this was a moment people talked about for years to come. The reaction from the crowd rivals some of the great sports moments in history.

Every era in this brief history had its big game, *Donkey Kong* in the 80s, *Street Fighter* in the 90s, and *Halo* in the 2000s. We went from stand-up arcade games to early consoles, which led to the boom of the sixth generation 128-bit consoles and ultimately the next-gen consoles and VR headsets. PC gaming began growing as well, and games like *Warcraft II* showed us what is possible with multiplayer gaming on a local area network and online.

StarCraft, made by Blizzard Entertainment, was without doubt the defining force in esports the early 2000s. Released in 1998, *StarCraft* almost instantly became a massive hit with competitive gamers. It helped that Blizzard built *StarCraft* with what they called a ladder system to facilitate competitiveness, with players vying for ranks. Eventually, these ladder systems were enhanced, and top players identified. Blizzard naturally wanted to develop this into some sort of a tournament, and did. *StarCraft* tournaments became a major attraction, particularly in countries like South Korea, where with millions of dollars in prizes, they, were televised and attracted thousands of viewers. The *StarCraft* League and now the Global *StarCraft II* League are still a major force in competitive gaming. Now one of the best-known video game companies, Blizzard's games all have an esports element.

This brings us to 2010 and the start of the esports explosion. It was obvious that esports a big deal—not just for gaming but for business. One of the largest corporations in the world, Amazon, owns Twitch, the premier streaming platform. Twitch is like the ESPN of esports, and anyone can produce live content on the platform. The biggest game companies in the world are focusing their development projects on games with a competitive element and then building the structure to host major tournaments. The development cycle of almost every game now involves deep multiplayer integration and at least a few boardroom discussions about how the game can be leveraged for competitive gameplay. We didn't get here by chance though. Once the big companies with big budgets, stepped in, there was little doubt where things were heading.

If the modern era of competitive gaming started with real-time strategy games such as *Warcraft* and *StarCraft* playing center stage, today the stage belongs to multiplayer online battle arena, or "MOBA," games. Now, *League of Legends, Dota, Smite*, and others are all hosting massive tournaments with huge prizes. The winners of these tournaments don't just go on to celebrity in the gaming space but are increasingly becoming celebrities in other pop culture realms as well. It's not uncommon for the winners of major tournaments like the *Fortnite* World Cup, or *League of Legends* World Championship to be interviewed on major television networks and make appearances on morning shows. The first *Dota 2* International, the world finals for *Dota*, was held in 2011 and has become a major international annual tournament.

You can't talk about competitive gaming without also mentioning some of the faces on the scene now. Possibly the largest personality is Tyler "Ninja" Blevins, a competitive *Fortnite* player and popular livestreamer. Ninja streams *Fortnite* and other games daily, sometimes for up to twelve hours a day, and he has hosted major celebrities such as Drake to play alongside him. The emergence of Ninja played a massive role in the emergence of *Fortnite* itself.[16] These popular livestreamers are critical to the cachet of esports and the games we choose to play. Ninja is a hero to a lot of kids in the same way that sports heroes from decades past are admired by adults.

Case in point: In 1993, Joe Carter hit one of the most iconic home runs in the history of baseball to win the World Series for the Toronto Blue Jays. I remember exactly where I was and exactly what I was doing at that moment, and so do a lot of people my age. It's a moment I will never forget. But my son is eleven years old and, for him and the millions of kids all around the world who just don't connect to baseball, football, hockey, or any other sport, these moments don't resonate. What does resonate with them is the team that wins the *League of Legends* World Championship. Ask them to talk about Fnatic, Cloud9, or Invictus, and they'll go all day. Ask them their thoughts on the *Fortnite* tournaments or the *Overwatch* World Cup, and you can't shut them up. These games, tournaments, and personalities make up their Joe Carter home-run moments.

The world is changing, and with it, the definition of sport. The history of esports is still being written, with its greatest moments probably yet to come. I'm excited to see what happens next, but one thing's for sure: esports is not going away. It's time for educators to get on board and bring its many benefits to students.

ROADBLOCKS TO IMPLEMENTATION

And all that history brings us to the present day. When the notion of adding esports to a school's extracurricular program is first broached, esports supporters typically hear a range of negative responses from edu-cators. For example, some teachers and administrators object to adding esports as an extracurricular activity, rightly pointing out that only a few participants will go on to become professional gamers. While this is true, society doesn't stop traditional young athletes from dreaming that dream, so why stop esports athletes? Even if they don't go pro, esports athletes—just like the many thousands of middle and high school ath-letes in other sports who don't become professional athletes—will learn a great deal and enjoy all the same benefits a traditional athlete gets from participating in sports. They may even earn a scholarship, or at the very least, improve their chances of getting into a college. In addition, esports offers many opportunities for participation beyond being a player.

Other times the responses are a little more biting:

"So, like sitting around playing video games?"

"I would hardly call that an athlete."

Hysterical laughter followed by, "Like Tetris? What a joke!"

"Seriously, you are going to spend money on that?"

These educators, who are highly skilled, normally compassionate, and leaders among their colleagues mean no ill intent. They simply don't understand because no one has ever taken the time to inform them. They are uneducated, and this book is here to help educate them. We talk extensively about these objections and how to respond to them in chapter 2.

Often lost in the debate about esports are the tremendous social and emotional positives associated with gaming. Set aside for the moment how an esports team would put your school and students one step ahead, and ignore the huge sums of scholarship money out there. Esports is not about being "cool" by allowing kids to play video games. It is about pro-viding kids with an opportunity they deserve to have. It's about engaging the kids who feel like they don't fit in. It is about giving every child an equal chance to participate. Whether you are a boy, a girl, nonbinary, het-erosexual, homosexual, physically handicapped, emotionally challenged, learning disabled, struggling with mental illness, homeless, homebound, receiving free/reduced lunch doesn't matter. Everyone is equal when it comes to participating in esports (though it's true that those without access to gaming at home can come into school programs with a disadvantage). What's remarkable about esports is how it gives each student a chance to play and participate with their peers and build relationships in ways that may not be possible when playing alone at home. It is about encouraging others to celebrate students who may not get the MVP trophy playing traditional sports.

CUT SCENE

FROM GRIDIRON GREAT TO ESPORTS COACH

As you may know, many professional athletes are avid gamers. In April 2020, we even saw the first *NBA 2K* Players Tournament, in which some of the best basketball players in the world competed for the title of best basketball video game pro athlete. But one athlete took his love of gaming a step further. Ahman Green, a four-time Pro Bowl running back and all-time leading rusher for the Green Bay Packers, showed that even professional athletes can turn a passion for esports into a career. Upon retiring from the NFL, Ahman returned to his roots and spent nearly a decade coaching high school football. But as a self-proclaimed passionate gamer, he couldn't quite shake his love of esports, as both a fan and a competitor. He began hosting an esports talk show and learning everything he could about the industry. In early 2020, his two passions converged, and Ahman was named esports coach at Lakeland University in Wisconsin. As coach of a growing program, Ahman can see clearly the direct parallels between his days playing and coaching football and his work in esports. In particular, there are a number of commonalities with the mental preparation required in the two sports. "On day one, I start a conversation with my students about how to lose in esports," he has said. "My coach at Nebraska, Frank Solich, used to tell me, 'Ease the mind.' He said, 'If you're anxious, if you're nervous, that means you're thinking about the game. That means you're mentally ready to play, and you're just waiting for the action to happen now. Your brain is going.' "

But the similarities don't stop there. Ahman has found that success in esports requires the same level of commitment that traditional sports demand of their players. As Ahman puts it: "Esports does require that same commitment. You have to practice and recover your mind and your body. You have to get sleep, you have to recover the right way, and you have to have, overall, physically good health. You gotta have a nice regimen as a gamer, just like you had to have a good regimen as an athlete to train for your sport."

As far as esports athletes playing at the collegiate level on scholarships like their traditional-sport peers, Ahman preaches patience. "Have a little bit more patience with college esports because it's so brand new. I have a lot of kids that I've recruited or who have reached out to me, and they're asking for esports scholarships. A lot of universities don't have esports scholarships. They have scholarships for the sports that have been around for one hundred years, like football, baseball, basketball, hockey, and softball. So I tell them that there may not be scholarships at all schools designated for esports now, but there will. Have patience."

But perhaps most importantly, Ahman noted how the skills required to be successful in esports are the same as those necessary to be a successful professional athlete. "Hard work in football and esports mirror each other. Outworking your opponent can help win more games overall. Dedication is a skill that means you will do anything and everything to help your team win in a positive way. Hold yourself to be accountable. Individuals don't win games . . . teams do. You must learn how to be accountable to the people around you."[17]

The goal of this book is simple. We believe educators have a responsibility to invest both mentally and financially in esports, as it provides a unique opportunity for students to be successful, not only on the field of play, but in life. Unlike other sports, the justification and road map for doing so haven't existed—until now. This book is designed to fill the gap and offer a helpful how-to manual for educators who are interested in trying to add esports to their extracurricular offerings and must be able to constructively respond to objections.

Those of you who have no idea what esports is and why you should know, you're in the right place. (In fact, we have a glossary of terms in the back, in case some of the terminology in the book seems like a foreign language.) If you've heard of esports and have been looking for information on how to get started with your own program, we've got you covered. Maybe you've already started implementing esports in your school and are looking to up your game with some tips and tricks. You'll find those in this book, as well. But our main objective here is to provide educators with information on how they can provide opportunities for every student to feel a sense of belonging and success. Esports has been a blessing to students and families who have struggled to find ways to connect with their school communities. Each one of us knows this because we've lived it ourselves, making us uniquely suited to write this book.

ESPORTS AND THE AUTHORS

Chris's Story

In 1998, when I was in eighth grade, Blizzard released *StarCraft*. *StarCraft* was my introduction to esports. My friends and I would bring our computers to each other's houses and play *StarCraft* after school or sports practice. It wasn't long before *StarCraft* blew up around town, and the local computer store started to host *StarCraft* LAN (local area network) tournaments. My friends and I would play in as many tournaments as we could.

Even when we didn't win, we still loved the competition and cheering for each other.

Flash-forward to 2011, when I went to my first professional esports tournament, a *StarCraft II* tournament at Caesars casino in Atlantic City. My friends and I, the same friends I'd been playing games with since 1998, decided to check it out. The tournament had light effects, smoke machines, entrance music, walkouts, jumbotrons, and livecasting. The capacity crowd knew every player by name and chanted and cheered for their favorite players. It was awesome. I never knew esports existed on that level.

I was a three-sport athlete in high school, played sports in college, and by 2011, I'd already been teaching and coaching varsity football, wrestling, and track for five years. I'd also played video games competitively since *StarCraft* in 1998. I've had a foot in both the esports and traditional sports world, and that 2011 tournament was a wake-up call: I was determined to help bring esports to education. Seven years later, I finally got the chance.

In September 2018, after six months of planning, my school district approved the creation of my FH Knights esports team.[18] The FH Knights were the first middle school esports team in the country, willing to play whoever we could schedule. As we were the first middle school, there were no other middle schools for us to play, so I reached out to Rutgers University to see if they would play us. To my surprise, they agreed. The first middle school esports match ever was against a college. We got our doors blown off but had a blast. Even though we got trounced, a middle school team taking on a college team got a lot of coverage in the press. My kids and I did some interviews, including with NBC and PBS.[19]

Flying high on that coverage, I reached out to a friend, Steve Isaacs, who had a video game club at his middle school. I asked him if he could put together a *Rocket League* team to play against my kids. A couple weeks later, the first true middle school versus middle school match was held. We played each other a few more times that year, and my team played another middle school from Pennsylvania, inspired by us to start their own team. We've grown as a team in the years since, and now there are dozens of teams around the world that we can face off against. There have been tremendous highs on this journey and more than a few roadblocks, and what I know now could fill a book! That's what you have in your hands right now—the guide I wish I'd had back in 2011.

Steve's Story

My days of gaming date back to my Atari 2600 and my Apple II Plus computer. Playing games was incredibly exciting, especially as a social outlet with friends, in both cooperative and competitive roles. Getting a new cartridge and running home to pop it into the console was such a rush! Over the years, I moved on to all the famous consoles: Intellivision; Sega Genesis and Dreamcast; PlayStation 1, PlayStation 2, and the PS4; Nintendo 64, GameCube, and Switch; and all the Xbox platforms.

I would get together with friends to play. Sports games were especially fun to play against one another, and we would set up tournaments and leagues. We played sports outside too, but I wasn't a stellar athlete. However, I could hold my own in *Tecmo Bowl* for sure. My college apartment became the *Tecmo Bowl* stadium (much to the dismay of my roommates). We would crowd around the console and play well into the night.

Those days defined my youth, years before the term "esports" was coined. There were probably some large-scale competitions in those days, so competitive gaming existed, but it hadn't truly come into its own (yet!).

I started my career in 1992, in Montclair, New Jersey, teaching students with special needs in a science and technology magnet school. I quickly saw how technology and games fit into learning, and that helped me personalize learning experiences for my students. I became friendly with Paul Tarantiles, our technology director at the time. Paul and I spent many lunch periods talking about ways to use technology creatively, as a learning tool. In time, our wives joined forces with us to open a technology training center. The primary business would be summer camps, and we also planned to offer after-school classes, services for schools, and adult training. We would often open on school holidays as a drop-in program for kids.

I quickly realized that gaming, technology, and learning could work beautifully together. Among our camp offerings were sessions that mixed games and learning. For example, one camp used the real-time strategy game *Age of Empires* to explore different civilizations. Campers would research the different strengths and deficits of their civilization and later apply this information as part of their strategy in the game. Students would spend the week becoming experts as they battled the other civilizations in the game. We also began to offer courses in computer programming and game design and development. It was very exciting to see kids get excited about creating their own content.

Then one day, something happened that changed my life. One of the kids brought in a copy of a game called *Warcraft II*. He mentioned that multiple people could play this game together over our network. The first time I saw us connect through LAN and play a game together on separate computers over our network was a transformational moment for me. This was my introduction to multiplayer gaming. Life as I knew it would never be the same.

We tried opening the store up on weekend evenings as an internet café, but it never took off. Instead we discovered that parents were looking for a safe space where their kids could come and meet their friends and play games over our network. Playing in the same building provided a great opportunity for kids to have a place they could call their own and hang out with their like-minded friends. (It didn't hurt that parents saw this as a safe place for their kids to hang out while they went out to dinner on a Friday night!) Things evolved quickly into team-based games, in which each team would sit together in one area of our center and play against the other team. There was something thrilling about playing in the same building and jumping up and high-fiving each other when something good happened, and even noodling the other team after a well-contested match.

As I continued my journey in gaming, I saw the game industry start booming. A few years ago, articles started appearing about students earning college scholarships for competitive gaming. At that moment, I knew we had arrived. Selling the idea of esports to school districts certainly hasn't been without its challenges, but this was certainly a good selling point!

In 2017 I started a game club at William Annin Middle School, where I teach. The description indicated that this would be a casual social club that would include opportunities for competitive gaming (esports). In 2018, our esports journey began when Chris Aviles called looking for middle schools to play against. When I approached my students, they were thrilled to have the opportunity to play against another school and we "leveled up" our game club to include a legitimate esports component. This led to several tournament-style matches with a few different schools. Students were exposed to competitive gaming, and we had Topher Jaims shoutcasting the action, adding quite an element of excitement. As we moved forward, many students had an opportunity to try their hand at shoutcasting with Topher, and eventually on their own. This year, we broke into two separate clubs: a casual gaming club and a competitive esports club. Both provide an important outlet for our students.

In 2018, I approached the principal of our high school, Ridge High School, who agreed it was important for our high school to participate in esports. Students play a big part in organizing the club, and it provides opportunities for competitive gamers, as well as others who want to be involved in the space. We have students working on graphic design, creating flyers, logos, and designs for our jerseys. We have others involved in marketing, and we plan to create opportunities for shoutcasting, as well. The esports coach, Justin Satter, a science teacher at the high school, treats it like any other sport, with a regular practice schedule. He also has networked extensively with other teachers in New Jersey to create additional interscholastic opportunities for his students.

When Chris pitched me the idea of writing a book about esports and schools, I was delighted to share the hard-earned wisdom of the past couple of years running my club and helping the high school team grow. Like him, I wished there had been a book like this to help me!

Christine's Story

I am not a gamer. The last video game I played was *Duck Hunt* on my original Nintendo in the 90s (which I still have, and if you bang the top of the machine enough, it still works). I have no personal interest in the games or consoles at all. Instead, my interest in esports stems from being a middle school administrator and thinking about kids who feel like they belong because we were willing to take a chance on an esports program. Recognizing that it is a growing field, I believed that it was important for our school to provide our students with an opportunity to participate in what might be their "thing." Like a soccer player shines on the soccer field and a singer shines on stage, our gaming students can shine if we provide the opportunity, which I believe is a critical mission. It was time to connect those students with a group of peers who shared their interests, spoke their language, and engaged in similar opportunities to play, and to highlight that as a victory to our school community.

I knew it would be a journey to weave esports into the culture of a small K–8 school district that was deeply rooted in its traditions. I started with my school's leadership team to "sell" the idea of an esports team. At first it was challenging. I was asking the district to invest money in what they perceived as "playing video games." So I dug deeper. I presented my colleagues with statistics about college scholarship opportunities, careers in professional gaming, viewership for matches, and how esports was holding its own against the likes of MLB and the NFL. I shared the social emotional learning (SEL) benefits of hosting a program and the ways it would build camaraderie among our students. After hearing all this and more, my administrative colleagues were not only on board—they were excited.

The middle school principal was thrilled. He saw this as an opportunity to provide students who may not identify with any of our existing cocurriculars a place and group in which they felt a sense of belonging. He was excited to show the school community how esports could be a means to build relationships and pride for what may be an underserved student population. He also saw it as an opportunity for inclusivity for our students. Regardless of whether a student is physically challenged, learning challenged, socially challenged, or none of the above, esports was an opportunity to level the playing field and offer equal opportunity to all.

In an effort to "do it right," I insisted that our esports program be recognized as an equal sport to all of our other sports. Of course, as with any unbudgeted request, funding is always an issue. The superintendent, who is always very supportive of new initiatives, especially ones that represent inclusion for our diverse student body, was totally on board. If I could find a way to fund the necessary equipment, the district would find the funding for the coach's stipend.

So I began my creative budgeting process. I worked with funding I had from an after-school program that was run by the district and was able to purchase five high-end gaming chairs. I also was able to multipurpose our three existing gaming PCs and applied to our education foundation for a grant to support the purchase of two more machines so that I could round out a team of five for our esports program. The grant was accepted, the chairs were purchased, and we were ready to get the ball rolling.

But at this point, the proverbial esports "ball" came to a screeching halt. Unfortunately, in mid-October, the district had a tremendous number of unforeseen costs surface. As with any small district, we needed to find a way to absorb their impact. And as you may have guessed, one of the victims of these unforeseen costs was the coach stipend that we would "find a way to fund." As a result, the esports coaching position was put on hold, along with the whole program. Then our staff learned of the new stipend for the esports coach. Many of them were bewildered by the concept of paying an adult a sizable stipend to supervise children who were playing video games. Luckily, having gone through the process already, I was able to easily explain the many benefits to offering esports as one of our competitive sports programs.

I must have been convincing, because it was music to my ears when our basketball coach articulated his interest in giving up basketball to coach an esports team. After my shock wore off, I said, "I had no idea you are a gamer." He replied, "I'm not, at all. I just really like what this is all about." That comment validated all the effort to bring esports to the district. The journey is far from over, but one thing I know for sure: I wish I'd had access to this book as I developed my vision and mission for the program in my district.

Jesse's Story

While I've been a pretty avid gamer my whole life, as I look back on my experiences with gaming, I realize the seeds of esports and competitive gaming were always there—even when the games themselves didn't necessarily allow for it. Of course, I grew up in arcades, pumping quarter after quarter into games like *Dig Dug*, *Galaga*, and *Tron*, as well as playing the systems I owned at home, like Atari (weirdly, I had the more unusual 5200 rather than the 2600 unit that everyone seemed to own) and a Nintendo Entertainment System (which I would sneak out of my closet for late-night *Legend of Zelda* sessions). But I knew my imagination to take things even further and my competitive nature extended beyond the limited capabilities of the game.

Even though I competed in some industry-standard gaming competitions (see embarrassing story in the Cut Scene earlier in this chapter), my real passion lay in sports gaming. Back then, it was rare for some of the earlier cartridge-based games to keep track of statistics. And even the ones that did some form of tracking used passcodes that simply tracked win-loss records. My middle school friends and I needed something more. The Sega Genesis classic *Lakers vs Celtics and the NBA Playoffs* captured our passion for sports, but since it didn't keep stats, we would record all of the games on VHS cassettes and then rewatch them to manually tabulate all the statistics, maintaining them ourselves. Playing as the Phoenix Suns in our fictional league, I was able to lead our league in scoring using the infamous Tom Chambers double-pump dunk from the three-point line that, to this day, I will argue is the most unstoppable scoring play in video game basketball history.

By high school I was able to run wild and break records with the legendary Bo Jackson in *Tecmo Super Bowl*. But as the technology evolved, so did our needs. By the time I was in college, sports games like the *Madden* series kept track of win-loss records and stats, but we were still constrained by the physical nature of the cartridge. In order to run a league with friends, with each one controlling a team, we needed to literally create a schedule for playing games, trading the cartridge from person to person. But the takeaway here is that there was always a desire, not just my own, but also friends', to elevate the competition in our gameplay.

Fast-forward from college through a twenty-year career as a technology consultant for Fortune 500 companies, a classroom teacher, and a director of technology and innovation for a public school district, and my interests stayed aligned with those of my younger self. The question I kept asking myself was: How can we find new and innovative ways to empower our learners in school? Clearly, technology has come a long way since I was in school (and even from only a handful of years ago). Christine and I formed Ready Learner One, an innovative learning solutions provider, with our good friend and colleague Dr. Micah Shippee with the idea of focusing our efforts on K–12 schools and helping educators incorporate emergent technologies into their pedagogy. Mainstream adoption of new technologies can be a slow build and take many years. While many schools have early adopters and pioneers who pave the way, many educators often need to learn and gather information before attempting to integrate new technologies into their teaching. We wanted to find a way to simplify and help accelerate that process.

We started with the exciting work being done in virtual and augmented reality. In early 2020, we released *Reality Bytes: Innovative Learning Using Augmented and Virtual Reality*, a book focused on explaining how the futuristic-seeming functions and uses provided by virtual and augmented reality could be used to create an impact in every classroom today. And in an era when we are being forced to quickly adopt remote learning out of necessity, these technologies have become even more appealing, providing access to teaching and learning outcomes that would not have been possible otherwise. But along with our work in AR and VR, another area jumped out at us: esports.

It's hard to find anyone who doesn't love playing games. Almost every parent and educator recognizes the important role that games can play in learning, from imaginary playground games to gamification in the classroom. But the idea of video games in school was quickly dismissed for a number of reasons (which we outline and provide counterpoints to later in the book). Meanwhile, esports was continuing to grow in popular culture, transitioning from a curiosity into something much more powerful: A new sport that threatened to overtake traditional sports in both popularity and viewership. And one thing that we recognized immediately was that esports, unlike pretty much every other sport, offered a unique opportunity for every student to be an active and engaged participant. Instead of relying solely on athletic ability, these esports gamers could be any gender, athletes or nonathletes, experienced or newbies, affluent or less privileged. Esports was the first new opportunity to enter education in a long time that could prove to be a great equalizer. Surely schools could benefit from noticing the changing landscape around esports and finding ways to tap into the needs and passions of their students—right?

As we started our research, Christine and I began talking to Steve and Chris. Steve had been a contributing writer in *Reality Bytes* and was well known for his work in both the VR and esports spaces. Chris was an educator Christine and I knew from the conference circuit and whose work, which we greatly respected, was well known. As we started sharing the work we had done as well as discussing our interests and ideas around esports, the partnership seemed like a perfect fit, and our collaboration on this Ready Learner One book was a no-brainer.

While we all played a number of roles in developing this book, one of my primary contributions, and a great privilege, was interviewing dozens of educators, students, gamers, and professionals to pick their brains and bring their stories and, more importantly, advice to this project. And what I came away with boiled down to this: esports is going to have a bigger impact on schools and society than we can imagine. And trust me, I can imagine quite a bit. But looking past the inspirational stories and best practices, it was clear that esports has changed the opportunities that school brings to the table for many of our students. Those who couldn't find a path for themselves now find that school is a place where they not only belong but can thrive. And isn't that the point of school, after all?

DESIGN OF THE BOOK

We hope that hearing our stories and reading this book assure you that no matter what your background, you can implement esports at your school, and your entire school community can rally around and participate in it. In this book you'll learn about all the different ways esports can benefit every student and provide a foundation for social and career success. Our goal is to give you practical insight into how any educator can get involved with esports. We recognize that not every educator comes to esports with the same level of experience and knowledge, so throughout the book we've included "Tips from the Field"—practical advice you can use to help you create your program—as well as "Cut Scenes"—stories from educators that we hope will inform and inspire you.

- Chapter 1, **The Why of Esports in Schools**, examines the many benefits that an esports program confers on participants through the lens of social and emotional learning (SEL). It both describes typical approaches and outcomes of SEL, and details what an SEL curriculum for esports should entail, cataloging the overall benefits of esports for students.

- Chapter 2, **Changing Perceptions about Esports**, lays out common objections to the formation of esports teams at public schools and offers a range of responses that organizers can offer naysayers.
- Chapter 3, **Working with Stakeholders**, explains how esports organizers should advocate for the sport when approaching stakeholders and offers a number of helpful talking points.
- Chapter 4, **Designing an Esports Program**, describes best practices for setting up, managing, and running an esports program, with particular attention to differences between club and varsity teams.
- The Conclusion, **Looking to the Future**, explores some possible developments in the world of esports.
- Recognizing that some educators may need additional support in getting started, we've also added a helpful **Appendix**, where we introduce our readers to an organization—the North American Scholastic Esports Federation (NASEF)—whose mission is to support the integration of esports into K–12 education. We take a closer look at that organization's curricula for play-based learning and end by suggesting several other possible partners for developing K–12 esports programs.

We hope you're ready to blast off into a journey exploring one of the most unique and exciting innovations to occur in the educational space in years. Here we go!

THE WHY OF ESPORTS IN SCHOOLS

E sports lends tremendous value to teaching and learning in schools. It is a great opportunity to teach students many different soft skills that are undeniably critical for future success, such as leadership, communication, teamwork, and sportsmanship. However, probably the most beneficial lessons that come from esports are those around social and emotional learning (SEL), both for the participating athletes and for the school community that surrounds them.

WHAT IS SOCIAL AND EMOTIONAL LEARNING AND WHY IS IT IMPORTANT?

According to the Collaborative for Academic, Social, and Emotional Learning (CASEL), "Social and emotional learning (SEL) is the process through which children and adults understand and manage emotions, set and achieve positive goals, feel and show empathy for others, establish and maintain positive relationships, and make responsible decisions."[1] Research has shown that students who participate in an SEL curriculum can improve academic performance, classroom behavior, ability to manage stress and depression, and attitudes toward self, others, and school.[2] In addition to the immediate benefits seen in the classroom, there are many long-term benefits to SEL. According to CASEL, students participating in programs using these types of curricula often see positive impacts on things like academics, conduct issues, emotional distress, and drug use, up to nearly two decades later.[3]

While support for SEL programming is overwhelming, often schools are concerned about budgets, program funding, etc. With this in mind, it is important to remember that some programs have resulted in an eleven-to-one return on investment.[4] For an even longer-term public financial impact, consider that SEL can decrease an individual's need to rely on public assistance, and lessen the chance of their being involved with police before adulthood and of spending time in the corrections system.[5]

The impact SEL programs have on academic and school performance are great reasons to include them in a curriculum, but consideration must also be given to students' futures. In a highly competitive job market, educators strive to do everything possible to set students up for success. SEL is an avenue to successful outcomes postgraduation. With employers such as Allstate, Bank of America, and Google looking at SEL competencies in employees, it would be negligent to not address these skills starting early. Consider that, according to CASEL, "six of the Top 10 skills identified by the World Economic Forum involve social and emotional competence" and "92% of surveyed executives say skills such as problem-solving and communicating clearly are equal to or more important than technical skills."[6] With these facts in mind, it is imperative that SEL skills are taught with at least the same rigor as technical skills.

Social and emotional learning has long been incorporated into sports, and some argue that sports provide a unique and powerful avenue to teach SEL skills in a way that would be impossible in a classroom setting. The Aspen Institute has identified sports as a tremendous resource in teaching youths SEL skills and has directly charged coaches with the responsibility of including these skills.[7] But is there a place for teaching SEL skills in esports? We will explore how, just as in traditional sports, esports provides the chance to teach SEL skills in a meaningful and impactful way. Esports coaches should join the movement of teaching SEL skills through sport, just as traditional coaches have been doing for years.

The value of teaching SEL through esports is proven, but it isn't new. Mindfulness and SEL training are being done at the collegiate and pro level, so it is only natural that would trickle down to high schools and middle schools. With many K–12 schools identifying and deploying SEL curricula and instructional practices, esports can fall in line with existing efforts and strengthen avenues of support for the school community.

Some of the more advanced K–12 esports programs are starting to teach the impact of nutrition and exercise on improved performance, how students can avoid becoming triggered or playing "tilted," and how to handle toxicity.

SEL IN ESPORTS

Traditional sports have a long history of teaching SEL skills such as teamwork, communication, and personal assessment. What may come as a surprise to you is that esports can also teach these skills and is uniquely positioned to teach these skills to individuals who may not be interested, eligible, or able to participate in traditional sports. Through esports, the SEL skills taught through traditional sports are available to a much wider audience.

When esports are met with resistance from individuals who subscribe to a more traditional concept of education and sport, the ability of esports to teach SEL competencies, which in turn can improve classroom behavior and academic performance, can be a make-or-break selling point.

When Chris was working with stakeholders in his district to get his esports team approved, he committed to creating a comprehensive SEL curriculum that would be incorporated into the team's practices. This SEL curriculum was intended to tackle the concerns the board of education, and likely other stakeholders in the district, had about playing video games in school. This curriculum would address players' health and wellness as well as concerns such as screen time, in-game rage, and toxicity, with the goal of helping students make healthy choices.

To build this curriculum, Chris collaborated with school psychologist Dr. Matt Strobel. Matt brought a unique perspective, as he is a gamer as well as high-caliber jiujitsu athlete and has both a clinical and sports psychology background.

THE CURRICULUM: HOW TO TEACH SEL SKILLS AND WHAT SKILLS TO TEACH

According to Matt, when we think about SEL in esports, we should realize that esports can give students a sense of belonging as well as increase their skill acquisition. Matt believes a strong curriculum follows the CASEL guidelines for teaching SEL, providing a variety of teaching methods throughout the course of the program.

The curriculum he and Chris developed followed the CASEL recommendations:

> Effective SEL approaches often incorporate four elements represented by the acronym SAFE:
>
> - Sequenced: Connected and coordinated activities to foster skills development
>
> - Active: Active forms of learning to help students master new skills and attitudes
>
> - Focused: A component that emphasizes developing personal and social skills
>
> - Explicit: Targeting specific social and emotional skills[8]

Let's look at a breakdown of a sample lesson to illustrate how the SAFE elements are utilized to teach communications at an esports practice: An "Effective Communication" lesson starts with a recap of the prior lesson and ends with assigning homework to be addressed in the next lesson (Sequenced). During the lesson, athletes participate in two activities in which they move their bodies while following directions from group leaders or teammates (Active). At the end of the activities, the group processes their performance, identifies personal strengths and weaknesses, and reflects on how they can improve their communication skills (Focused). The entire lesson targets the ability to effectively communicate with teammates, friends, other peers, teachers, coaches, other adults, etc. (Explicit). This offline lesson can translate into improved communication in-game, as students will have prior experience taking direction from teammates and reacting appropriately.

The SAFE acronym guides how to teach SEL topics, but consideration must be given to what to teach. Many skills fall within the overarching theme of SEL. CASEL has identified five domains of social emotional learning: self-awareness, self-management, social awareness, relationship skills, and responsible decision-making. An effective esports curriculum should create lessons around all these domains, with every lesson in the curriculum targeting multiple CASEL standards.

Let's return to the Effective Communication lesson to see the five domains in action. It addresses self-awareness by helping esports athletes recognize their strengths and limitations as communicators; self-management by teaching players the importance of regulating their behavior in order to be effective communicators; social awareness by teaching how to accept supportive feedback from leaders and peers; and relationship skills by teaching how to communicate clearly and with purpose. Lessons about hate speech, bias, and cyberbullying primarily focus on responsible decision-making, but also teach how to be self- and socially aware, manage one's behavior, and build relationship skills with trusted peers. In addition to the lessons, esports athletes should keep a log in which they track goals based on the CASEL standards, taking the lessons out of the classroom and into their daily life.

Chris and Matt are acutely aware that esports athletes do not operate in a vacuum, so they advocate for a systems-level approach to teaching SEL skills. With the involvement of key stakeholders, the SEL message can be spread and supported in ways beyond only teaching lessons. Parent and staff workshops are part of the curriculum. The parent workshop provides an overview of the SEL curriculum and provides training on how to support athletes. The staff training is very similar to the parent training but also covers how the esports program will function in the educational environment.

Once there is a foundation of what SEL skills to teach in an esports program and how, further attention must be paid to the specific SEL skills that can be addressed through esports and how they relate to esports athletes. It is easy to envision how skills like leadership, teamwork, and communication can be improved through esports, but there is a lot more that can be done. Chris and Matt identified three domains of social and emotional learning that educators should be teaching through esports: skill acquisition, health and wellness, and navigating digital culture.

TIPS FROM THE FIELD

THE FIVE PILLARS

It can be easy to get lost in all of the research and stories about the various benefits that an esports program can provide to both students and schools, so James O'Hagan, director of digital and virtual learning for the Racine Unified School District, has identified what he calls the five "pillars," or key reasons for districts to adopt esports programs:[9]

- Esports helps to promote physical and mental health.

- Esports allows us to redefine our athletic culture.

- Esports diversifies opportunities for student participation.

- Esports increases collegiate scholarship pathways.

- Playing games is an important part of school.

It is important to keep these pillars in mind as you begin exploring the possibilities for establishing or enhancing a program in your own school or district. They also provide categories to help you collect your own ideas and articulate your plans and the benefits of your program. We will take a look at each of these ideas in this book.

Skill Acquisition: Communication

When considering skills that can be developed and enhanced by esports, the first concept that may come to mind is communication. Any effective esports team must communicate well while playing or their goals and objectives will not be met. While there are some logistical ways to enhance communication (e.g., having good headsets and ensuring that everything is working properly), more can be done. By providing direct teaching and coaching about communication skills, esports coaches can expect to see a positive outcome in performance.

Have you ever been in a conversation where everyone is talking at the same time trying to get their point across? How effectively did everyone communicate? Was anyone able to really make a point? Even if someone said something profound, did anyone hear them? Or was everyone too busy working to get their voice heard? By teaching skills for effective communication, coaches can train their athletes to listen to each other, work toward common goals, and use strategies that would be impossible if everyone were just shouting into their headsets.

An effective curriculum will have lessons in how to communicate clearly, with detail, using targeted and specific language, as well help athletes look at their current communication styles and adapt them to be more productive. These skills are taught through experiential learning: having players participate in games and activities and then studying their performance.

For example, in one activity an esports athlete is blindfolded and then tries to navigate a simple classroom obstacle course made up of desks with the help of verbal commands from the rest of the team. Players quickly learn that if they all shout commands at the same time, their teammate quickly runs into problems. They also learn the need to be specific ("take three big steps forward"), as vague commands ("go forward") lead to trouble. During the assessment part of the lesson, players analyze how their communication styles impacted their teammate in a real-life scenario. The goal is for students on your team to learn that it is better to take turns while speaking and be as specific as possible, skills that not only apply to communicating in esports, but to all aspects of life.

After the physical movement around the room, players take the activity into their chosen game. Two teams, each with one blindfolded member, compete. The sighted teammate tells the blindfolded team member what is going on in the game, where they are on the map, and what they need to do to win. Afterward, the team discusses what it was like to only listen or only communicate and what they realized about the synergy between listening and communicating.

Students will realize that communicating what they are seeing and what they are doing, rather than telling a teammate what to do, is a communication style that will lead to more wins than if they yell, talk over each other, and boss each other around. Like Chris tells the FH Knights, by the time you tell your teammate what to do—like "Get back to the goal!"—the moment has likely passed.

Teamwork

Another skill that is imperative for athletes to develop is teamwork. When everyone on a team works as an individual, the team will not succeed. However, by teaching athletes how to work together, you can help improve their performance. Through experiential learning, Chris and Matt teach strategies to develop a team mentality as well as foster positive relationships. Through self-exploration, team members learn what type of teammate they are and can work on becoming the type of teammate they hope to be.

These goals are accomplished through activities that combine physical movement and mental tasks. In these activities, players pull from their communication skills to problem solve and work effectively toward a common good. Athletes learn how to listen to others' opinions while expressing their own.

For example, in one mental task, teammates work together to place in rank order a list of items they would need in a survival situation. At the end of the activity the group leader facilitates a discussion, not about the correct rankings, but instead about how the team spoke with one another and how they worked to create one list from many.

Sometimes during an esports match, things go wrong. Another activity that helps students practice their teamwork skills is a scenario where the team leader's microphone malfunctions. If the primary communicator's (sometimes called the "shot caller") mic were to malfunction, who would step up? In this drill, players are expected to figure out on the fly, in the midst of competition, who will become the new shot caller to carry their team to victory. This is a great activity for an esports coach to spring on players unannounced in the middle of practice, since it comes with the added bonus of not just improving communication, but also helping students learn how to overcome adversity and be flexible in the roles they find themselves in . . . or are forced into.

Every team needs leaders and followers, and by learning about these roles and how they all work synergistically, the team will form and strengthen. From there, players make the logic leap that being a successful teammate and winning matches often has less to do with individual performance and more to do with putting the team before yourself as you work together to achieve a common goal.

Goal Setting

While communication and teamwork primarily focus on working with others, the skill of goal setting focuses on oneself. Goal setting teaches esports athletes the difference between performance and process goals and how to craft goals that are SMART (specific, measurable, attainable, relevant, and have a timeframe).[10] Once players learn how to set goals, they can use the skill to enhance all their other learning.

The next section of this chapter will discuss health and wellness, which includes some topics that are perfect for goal setting. Think about new year resolutions. How many stick? What would increase the odds of a resolution being kept? One could argue that if the resolution were a specific goal that was measurable while being attainable and relevant and had a timeframe around it, the likelihood of the resolution being followed would increase.

For example, maybe the resolution was to get in better shape. That doesn't say much about what the goal actually is. It also focuses on an outcome versus focusing on how to reach that end goal, which makes it difficult to follow. Now think about if the resolution was, "I will go to the gym to walk on the treadmill for at least thirty minutes two times per week for the month of January." That goal is specific (you are going to walk on a treadmill), measurable (at a minimum you could easily type a note into a calendar indicating the days you walked), attainable (assuming that you belong to a gym and have time in your schedule to go for thirty minutes twice a week), relevant (you want to get in better shape), and has a timeframe (thirty minutes, two times per week, for January). By learning how to craft SMART goals esports athletes learn a valuable skill that they can utilize in many aspects of life.

TIPS FROM THE FIELD

RECOGNIZING THE VALUE OF GAMES TOGETHER

It can be easy to fall into the trap of dismissing the value of games and esports without taking a look at the benefits they provide. But at the forefront of esports are students collaborating and working together toward common goals, many of which provide numerous SEL benefits. Mimi Ito, a cultural anthropologist, learning scientist, and founder of Connected Camps, tells us what she has found in her research:

> I think gaming communities and fandom communities have always been pushing the envelope for how peer-to-peer learning can happen in digital and network environments. We've run a lot of programs in, for example, *Minecraft* and

Roblox, as well as esports. These gaming communities and companies have realized that when they provide resources that allow players to create meaning, they develop games that are so complex you can't learn them unless you're learning with other players in sort of a collaborative and social way. Those are the things that I think have really put gaming communities at the forefront of online peer-to-peer learning. And then when esports started to rise as a genre of how people engage with games, it introduced this level of spectatorship and competition that created even more intensity in terms of our young people or players wanting to get better and to work hard. And so it added, in addition to just the knowledge economy around gaming, a kind of competitive teamwork component that I think really accelerated young people's engagement and the range of young people who want to participate, as players and as interpreters, spectators, screencasters, streamers—all of these other activities that young people can participate in has really expanded with esports.

Personal Awareness

As part of learning empathy, esports athletes must understand themselves in order to realize that others can share similar qualities. One way to achieve this is by participating in a personal experience exercise during which esports athletes respond to questions about themselves while observing who has had similar experiences.

This type of exercise is similar to a privilege walk,[11] where individuals work to realize what they have in common, as well as what sets them apart. While noticing what is similar is important as a step toward building trust and psychological safety, the main goal of this exercise is to help athletes realize that not everyone has the same background, and therefore it is unrealistic to expect everyone to be judged according to the same criteria. At a very basic level, understanding that we all have strengths and weaknesses can help teams develop and figure out roles. On a higher level, teams can start working toward furthering each other's strengths while compensating for weaknesses in others. Individuals can also work on correcting weaknesses by using other skills taught throughout the curriculum, such as SMART goals. The focus is also on learning that what is fair is not always equal, and that fairness means everyone gets what they need, which is rarely the same for each person. This exercise also helps to highlight that esports can be a sport for everyone, with individuals having unique roles (e.g., player, assistant coach, manager, statistician, equipment specialist). The adage "Everyone is a genius. But if you judge a fish by its ability to climb a tree, it will live its whole life believing that it is stupid" embodies the spirit of this lesson.

By participating in this exercise, esports athletes can learn that they are not alone in their feelings or experiences, and they can recognize ways that they are similar to each other that may not be initially obvious. Having made these types of connections, esports athletes can then use their personal experiences to understand the experiences of others, building empathy, teamwork, and mutual respect.

Sense of Belonging

When Chris first started his esports team, he was surprised to see who came out. Not a single student was playing a sport, nor did they have any home-school connection. They weren't involved in any clubs either. Mostly the kids went home after school every day and played video games by themselves. The best part about starting the esports team was watching the kids develop a sense of belonging. Instead of playing alone like before, the kids now generally game together outside of school. After matches, they often go out for a slice of pizza together. It is the sense of community and belonging that is esports's greatest strength, since the kids who may need to feel like part of something the most aren't getting that need met elsewhere.

Facilitating this sense of belonging through an esports curriculum is most meaningfully accomplished by creating a code of conduct—rules on how your team will conduct themselves that focus on respect for diversity and inclusivity. By creating a code of conduct, preferably with your team, that includes discussing the importance of the esports team being a welcoming, safe space for all people, we can begin to have conversations with students about how every member of the team is valuable and brings something unique to the team. Additionally, it is important to go beyond passive rules about how athletes treat each other. Incorporating bystander intervention training is a great way to help students learn how to take an active role in policing their esports team and keeping it a safe place for everyone.[12]

There are a few key noncurricular ways to facilitate this sense of community. The symbolism that is represented in having team jerseys is powerful. Watching the athletes walk down the halls collecting high fives in their sweet-looking esports jerseys evokes a sense of pride for all members of the school community. For my team, students submitted ideas for the team jersey, contacted jersey makers to get quotes and samples, and ultimately voted on the jersey they liked the best for their team.

Second, even though esports matches are played online and with each team at their respective schools, it is important for esports coaches to turn match day into an event. Just like traditional sports, esports matches should be open to other students, teachers, and parents. Having a crowd coming to watch the match and support the team feels just as good to esports players as it does traditional athletes.

Finally, it is important to have high expectations for the athletes. Having high expectations means tying eligibility to attendance, behavior, and (sometimes) grades. If students don't show up or act appropriately, they can be benched, suspended, or removed from the team. Having high expectations also means treating the esports athletes the same as traditional athletes. By encouraging and challenging them, a coach shows how much they care about and believe in team members. Having team rules around attendance and behavior shows the athletes that you take esports and their presence on the team seriously. It lets them know you value them, and you will only accept their best.

HEALTH AND WELLNESS

When we think about esports, health and wellness may not be the first concepts that come to mind. The stereotype of a gamer sitting in a dark room consuming snack foods and energy drinks at all hours may be what you're more likely to imagine when you hear "esports athlete." While this may be a true depiction of some gamers, it is the furthest thing from the truth for elite esports athletes. Just like successful traditional athletes, esports athletes require their bodies to perform at the highest level.

If you think about it, a successful esports athlete's body must be able to endure hours in essentially one position, while their mind must make an infinite number of decisions in split seconds. These facts, coupled with the exceptional fine motor skills required to operate a controller or keypad, start to paint the picture of esports athletes having health and wellness needs very similar to those of traditional athletes. With this in mind, any quality curriculum should include lessons on how to take care of one's health and wellness. For example, Chris and Matt believe every esports curriculum should have lessons on diet, sleep, exercise, the effects of performance-enhancing substances, and mindfulness, which are all foundational skills for health and wellness.

Diet

Esports athletes should learn about healthy eating habits as a way to improve their overall well-being as well as their esports performance. Think about a time when you may have not been eating well—how did you feel? Maybe you felt physically or cognitively sluggish, uncomfortable, or unmotivated. Now think of times when you have been able to eat well. Maybe you felt healthier or energized. These are the feelings a successful esports athlete needs to experience on a regular basis.

By teaching esports athletes ways to eat a healthy diet, you can help them can improve not only as esports athletes, but in many domains of their lives. Nutrition can be a complex topic to address with students due to the variation in access that students have to different types of foods. Haylesh Patel, esports exercise physiologist at UCI, says the greatest factor that he has observed in young athlete's nutritional behavior is the influence at home of their parents and family. Patel says, "We tend to mimic the behaviors of those who greatly influence us, and generally speaking, it is our parents who we mirror as we grow."

Patel says there are a couple of ways esports coaches can try to shift focus of nutritional habits:

- Conduct a short workshop or seminar in which a dietitian talks about the effect of different food types on brain function (cognition) and overall health. Having parents present during this presentation could be helpful.
- Provide the students with tasty and healthy snacks and water during practices or matches.
- Provide examples of what professionals from the gaming and esports scene do.
- Provide nutritional information handouts or perhaps a sample weekly eating plan that has been created by a dietitian or nutritionist.

Sleep

Sleep is a necessity of life, and for athletes, getting the right quantity and quality of sleep is even more important. Esports athletes are no different. Sleep is necessary to recover from the physical, cognitive, and emotional tolls that gaming can take on the mind and body. Not getting the necessary quality or quantity can lead to cognitive and physical deficits, such as issues with physical health, mental health, and performance, including increasing the likelihood of accidents.

Being awake for twenty-four hours has been equated to having a blood alcohol limit of .10, over the legal limit for driving while intoxicated.[13] Although gaming while sleep deprived may not carry the same level of consequences as driving while drowsy, competitive esports athletes need to make every effort to be as successful as possible. Not getting enough sleep can impact performance in many ways.

Esports athletes should learn about the importance of sleep and then assess their current sleep quality and quantity. Through lessons woven into esports practice, these assessments are compared with medical recommendations, and discrepancies are examined. Esports athletes then work on a plan to increase the quality and quantity of their sleep until it meets recommendations. Examining sleep also leads to valuable conversations about screen time and its impact on sleep.

One of the most meaningful transformations Chris saw in a student was when he realized the impact that blue light—specifically the light emitted by computer screens, TVs, and phones—had on his sleep. Blue light, more than any other light, blocks the secretion of melatonin, the sleep hormone. Realizing his ability to fall asleep was likely being impacted by his gaming before bed, Chris's athlete started ending his gaming session an hour earlier than he had been and found himself falling asleep more easily.

Exercise

As mentioned before, a successful esports athlete's body must be able to endure hours of being in essentially one position while using exceptionally fine motor skills—challenges that regular exercise can help address. In addition to helping with esports performance, exercise has also been shown to improve mental health and mood, help thinking/learning/judgment skills, and improve sleep.[14]

As esports athletes participate in a sport that is more sedentary than most traditional sports, exercise needs to happen outside of time spent engaging in competition. By incorporating exercise as part of practices—including pregame stretching, physical activity during game breaks, and a cool down at the end of practice—as well as encouraging and educating athletes on effective exercise between practice sessions, coaches can help esports athletes gain the benefit of exercise in ways similar to traditional athletes.

Chris and Matt help their students first complete an assessment of their current exercise levels and then compare this data with recommended guidelines. Discrepancies are analyzed and plans are created to help esports athletes commit to exercising as part of their routines. In follow-up lessons, players report on their exercise habits and discuss them with their teammates and coaches.

CUT SCENE

AN SEL GOLDMINE!

Laurence Cocco, senior program consultant for the Sustainable Jersey Digital Schools Program and former director of educational technology for the New Jersey Department of Education, has been exploring the benefits of esports for quite some time, and has been a pioneer in advocacy for the recognition and inclusion of esports at the state level. Among the many reasons for his passion around this are the numerous SEL benefits provided by esports. As Laurence puts it:

> The SEL aspect of this is absolutely compelling and critical. This is a way to reach students who are not traditionally motivated, who were not motivated by traditional teaching methods, and who are not included in a sports program or a music program. I can't tell you how many times I've heard from educators about how they're getting the students that no one else has been able to reach.

> Schools like Lackawanna College have put in a series of requirements. Students have to get up and stretch and do exercises for a certain amount of time every time they're in the gaming

room. They have to put in enough hours at the gym. They have to keep an academic standard up. They have to keep their attendance record up. Student achievement is going through the roof. And attendance is going up. Tardiness is going down. Absenteeism is going down. They're motivating these students. They're happy, they're adjusted. And this is how we're reaching the part of the student population that to this date has been left by the wayside or has fallen through the cracks. So not only is it important from an SEL viewpoint, but it's important for the ability to have a career.

Performance-Enhancing Substances

In an unfortunate parallel to traditional sports, some esports athletes are turning to substances to increase their performance.[15] When huge payouts are on the line, esports athletes can fall into the same traps as traditional athletes. In an effort to teach responsible decision-making, coaches cannot turn a blind eye to the fact that some of their esports athletes may be considering, or are even already using, performance-enhancing substances.

Matt believes we need to tackle this unsettling reality by both addressing the topic head on, with a lesson about substance use, and indirectly, with lessons about wellness and how to naturally improve performance. Sports and substance use/abuse have a longstanding relationship (dating back as far as ancient Greeks in the Olympics and Roman gladiators[16]), and esports is no different. While the easy association is between sports and steroids, it is important to recognize that many types of substances are used by athletes to help with performance as well as personal issues both in and outside of sports (e.g., stress, relationship issues, pressure to perform, injury). This is also a complex issue, as it is not 100 percent clear how sports impact substance use for student athletes. In one study, some sports resulted in an increased use, while other sports had the opposite effect.[17] Furthering this issue is the fact that many student athletes are also at the age when experimenting with drugs and alcohol is considered the developmental norm. In addition, it has become clear that there is at least some use of stimulants by esports athletes as a way to gain a competitive advantage.[18]

Taking this all into account, it would be negligent to work with esports athletes, especially in this age bracket, and not address these issues. Chris and Matt tackle these concerns head on with lessons about the dangers of substance use, how to help a teammate who is using substances, and how to naturally improve performance and cope with stressors without using substances. These skills align with the performance triad (nutrition, sleep, exercise) to form a comprehensive package of skills that can help athletes overcome adversity and increase performance in ways that don't require artificial substances.

Mindfulness

Mindfulness has been proven to increase performance for many types of athletes, including Olympic BMX riders.[19] That fact, coupled with the concept that esports athletes share many similar traits with traditional athletes, makes clear that learning mindfulness skills can benefit esports athletes.

One way of teaching mindfulness is by explaining how to come back to the present moment when your thoughts drift to the future or the past. This has direct implications for gameplay, because if you are worried about what has already happened or anxious about what is going to happen, you will miss what is happening, resulting in being killed, goals being scored against you, etc.

Teaching esports athletes to focus on their breath is a start to teaching deeper mindfulness skills. As simple as it sounds, focusing on your breath is not easy at first. Esports athletes are taught how to let go of thoughts through a visualization activity and then bring their awareness back to their breath. They are first taught how to conduct an emotion scan in which they use physical cues to identify how they are feeling.

Next, they are taught the strategy of having a thought, visualizing the thought in a bubble, and then letting the thought float away. This is in direct contrast to what most athletes initially try, which is to suppress the thought—rarely, if ever, successful. Once athletes know how they are feeling and how to let go of thoughts, they then work on focusing on a stimulus, such as the sound of a bell, while letting go of their thoughts. Athletes are also taught how to "check it at the door," which is a strategy in which they focus on leaving anything that is on their mind outside of the practice area. By using all of these skills, athletes can enter a practice or competition setting and pay full attention to the task at hand. By learning these skills and then practicing them during gameplay, esports athletes can increase performance, not only during gaming, but across many domains in their lives.

Avoiding Burnout and Finding Balance

No conversation about health and wellness would be complete without addressing the concepts of avoiding burnout and finding balance. Esports athletes share similar stressors to traditional athletes and are not immune to burnout. In fact, many esports athletes retire long before traditional athletes would be old enough to make it into the major leagues.[20]

As part of a comprehensive SEL curriculum, it is important to teach about burnout while also providing guidance on avoiding it. Chris and Matt achieve this goal in two ways: by teaching skills that have been shown to prevent burnout (such as the other health and wellness skills) and by directly addressing the signs and symptoms of burnout.[21]

When provided knowledge about how to identify burnout, esports athletes can look out for symptoms within themselves, as well as look out for their teammates, and then use the skills they have learned to combat negative emotions.

The odds of becoming a professional athlete are slim, and the odds of becoming a professional esports athlete are similarly small.[22] This is a natural function of the competitiveness of the esports market.[23] Those odds, coupled with the fact that esports athletes often retire very young,

THE ESPORTS EDUCATION PLAYBOOK

provide the impetus to teach about finding balance. Any professional athlete performing at a high level must spend a lot of time honing their craft, and esports athletes are no different. By teaching esports athletes about finding a balance in life, coaches and other professionals have an opportunity to set them up for long-term success. Teaching balance includes discussing how each individual has many facets that make them who they are and that not finding success in one domain does not mean they are a complete failure. In the curriculum Chris and Matt developed, students first analyze the odds of becoming a professional esports athlete and learn about the difficult path to get there. They are then taught to identify all of the things that make them who they are and to celebrate that diversity. This allows for a broader sense of self that does not rely solely on success in one domain. By thinking about how a student may be an esports athlete but also a sister, daughter, math whiz, volunteer at an animal rescue, etc., the range of who the student is broadens and success can be found in any of these domains. Our chapter on different roles and esports careers is important to point out here, as many students may be excited to learn that they can have a lucrative, fulfilling career in esports without having to be a player.

NAVIGATING DIGITAL CULTURE

Although more tech savvy than their parents, kids today may find themselves in situations on the internet or while playing video games in which they may experience difficult-to-navigate negative interactions. We often hear about toxicity in gaming—expressions of homophobia, misogyny, racism, etc.—that our students may be exposed to while playing or interacting with others online. It is important that educators address the toxic aspect of digital culture head on, as an esports coach may be the only person in a student's life who is aware that these interactions happen.

As adults, we have an incredibly important yet difficult challenge teaching kids how to navigate the internet and understand internet culture. While an overwhelming majority of what goes on in social media—the comment sections of websites and forums like Reddit (which is a collection of online web forums where members can create and share content, as well as discuss that content, fandom, or interest)— is fine, if not downright boring, there is a toxic subsection of the internet that is full of horrible people. There are places that use meme culture to recruit kids into white supremacist groups, and places that celebrate school shooters and other acts of terror. It is our duty as teachers to help keep students safe and identify hazards.

An esports team, which is likely to be full of internet-savvy students, is a great place to tackle the tough but important cultural issues our students face on a regular basis that fly under most adults' radar. The usual digital-citizenship curriculum is not enough. We need to be there to help students unpack their experiences on the internet, and we need to model behavior to keep them safe. Esports is also a way to educate our most vulnerable students. In fact, that should be viewed as our responsibility. If we do not tackle these issues in school, we default to sending students home to often unsupervised gaming environments where they are subject to these challenges without the skills or support to handle them.

If we truly want to teach digital citizenship and nurture good digital responsibility, we need to see this as an opportunity, not a liability. Esports provides just that: an opportunity to set and enforce guidelines while also educating students about good sportsmanship. Toxicity has become quite a blemish on competitive gaming, but we can shift this, setting kids on the path to understanding how to handle difficult situations and changing the culture.

Digital Sportsmanship

In traditional sports, your opponent is physically present during the competition. This can differ with esports, as matches and tournaments can occur all over the world with teams on different continents. This adds a challenge when teaching about sportsmanship because of the physical disconnect between teams. A solid SEL curriculum should teach skills in a way that is not only applicable to the digital world, but also to the physical world.

Recall the prior discussion of communication skills. Are the skills taught for esports not also applicable to any conversation, whether taking place digitally across time zones and oceans or face-to-face across the dinner table? By directly teaching skills through esports, coaches have a real opportunity to impact esports athletes' abilities outside of the gaming world.

To help students understand that there are real people behind the screens and games they interact with, Chris instituted something he calls the virtual handshake. After a match, Chris's FH Knights will Skype their opponents and, win or lose, congratulate them on a good game, often written or expressed as GG in gamer culture. This allows for esports athletes to see the people they are playing, putting a face and name to the voices they heard through a headset. By seeing that there are real people, and often people similar to themselves, on the other end of the headset, esports athletes humanize their opponents, which can increase empathy. With increased empathy, esports athletes are more likely to treat opponents respectfully.

Dealing with Rage

Esports differ from traditional sports in the area of rage.[24] While it would be unusual to see a soccer player getting carded for screaming at his teammates throughout a match due to their performance (one coach said he had never seen this happen in over thirty years of coaching[25]), esports athletes have higher rates of showing rage toward each other. In fact, esports athletes are faced with having to deal with rage from other opponents, teammates, and themselves.

Rage has a direct impact on esports athletes' success and can often make or break an individual's or team's performance. Due to a unique need in this area, the SEL curriculum has lessons for esports athletes specifically tailored to rage or becoming triggered, as it is commonly referred to. As part of this lesson, esports athletes learn how to recognize precursors to rage and put a stop to the feeling before it starts.

Dealing with rage starts with learning how to identify early warning signs that can lead to that powerful emotion. As mentioned earlier, emotion scans are taught as a way for athletes to start recognizing how they are feeling. Without recognition, intervention is very difficult, which is why so much time is spent on this fundamental skill. The pace of play is a major challenge that esports athletes face. Many traditional sports provide opportunities to take a quick break and regroup (e.g., between downs in football, while you are playing defense in soccer but your striker has the ball, between heats in swimming), but esports offers little time to stop and think—and often if you try, you are out of the game by the time you tune back in! Esports athletes also do not usually have the chance to come off the field, speak with a coach, and rejoin the game. With all of this in mind, the curriculum Chris and Matt designed teaches athletes skills that they can use during gameplay, such as breathing, visualization, and positive self-talk (PST). Breathing and visualization have been discussed earlier in this chapter, but PST is a new skill. This strategy aligns with the work to prevent burnout in that it also addresses the fact that esports athletes are more than just players. Athletes are taught to quickly think in the moment of all of the other domains that they are successful in, as well as how it is objectively impossible to put a value on their gameplay, as the only way to possibly do this would be to break down every second the athlete ever played and determine the value of each second. Athletes also work on a personal mantra (the self-talk) to repeat internally while playing, such as "This game does not define me, my play does not define me, I am more than an athlete."

Hate Speech and Bias

Just like in the physical world, the digital world consists of all types of people. Esports athletes must learn to deal with the different types of players they come across in a similar fashion to traditional athletes. Where esports differs is in the use of the digital platform by groups supporting hate to spread their rhetoric and attempt to recruit members. (Though one could argue that this has also occurred in traditional sports: the 1936 Olympic games were used to promote Nazi ideals, sports were used as part of Hitler Youth indoctrination, and mixed martial arts are currently being used in some cases to recruit members for far-right groups.)[26] Regardless of the past, the current reality is that some nefarious players are using esports as a tool to spread hate and recruit vulnerable players into extremist groups, and it would be negligent to not address this issue in an SEL curriculum for esports.[27] This issue is so pervasive that it was even addressed by the creators of the Netflix series *Big Mouth* in an episode where one of the main characters, a middle school–aged boy, is recruited by a right-wing group after posting a video online in which he complains about his girlfriend breaking up with him.

You may think that identifying hate speech and recruitment efforts would be easy and that it is not worth teaching esports athletes this skill, however, even the United States Military Academy has been deceived by white supremacist rhetoric. The army football team used a slogan until December 2019 that originated in white supremacist gangs from the mid-1990s.[28] So the esports curriculum combats recruitment efforts, hate speech, bias, homophobia, and misogyny by teaching esports athletes skills such as how to identify, report, and respond to statements that fall within those categories. For example, the group will watch a video that discusses how to directly counter hate speech and then problem solve how they would respond if they were exposed to those types of statements while gaming. By tackling these topics head on, esports athletes learn powerful skills that will prevent them from being indoctrinated and provide learning that parents/guardians may not be able to provide because they are not knowledgeable about the digital landscape.

The first step in working with athletes who are being exposed to, or are even engaging in, hateful statements is identifying them. Chris and Matt pay particular attention to statements (through verbal communication, memes, messages, etc.) made by athletes. They also closely monitor players for changes in behavior. One of the best opportunities to identify students is during competition, when the stakes are high. This is often when a statement might be made that would be censored at other times. A great example is when you are driving. If someone cuts you off, what might you say or call that person? Esports adds a challenge in that the person receiving the insult is not physically present, which can contribute to the "keyboard warrior" mentality—it is easy to say things when there is no chance that the person can physically retaliate. Once students are identified, Chris and Matt work with them on understanding. Does the athlete know what they said do they know what it means? Depending on the outcome of this inquiry, a plan can be created to help the athlete learn from their mistakes. Sometimes this involves reaching out to parents and connecting the family with professional mental health providers who can work with this topic.

Mark Deppe, an esports commissioner for NASEF, stated, "When I look at esports, I see it as uncharted territory, and there is risk involved, but that's when you find the reward as well."[29] Social and emotional learning provides an opportunity to capitalize on some of the rewards. SEL lessons can mitigate some of the potential risks and provide skills that go far beyond the esports domain. By combining teaching esports athletes how to be better at esports with SEL lessons designed to teach esports athletes how to be better people, we can provide skills and knowledge to a group of students who may not have had any other way to access this material. Esports can serve as a gateway to learning SEL skills that were once only available to students who participated in more traditional sports.

TIPS FROM THE FIELD

GAMING AS MODEL FOR LEARNING

In his book, *WanderlustEDU: An Educator's Guide to Innovation, Change, and Adventure*, Dr. Micah Shippee wrote extensively about the power of gaming in the classroom as a vehicle for providing deep and meaningful learning experiences. A key takeaway was that in order to achieve the benefits provided by games in the classroom, the educator need not be a gamer themself.[30] But by simply taking advantage of the inherent benefit that games offer in an instructional setting, educators can accomplish the following goals:

- Modeling innovation

- Modeling failure and resilience

- Building empathy and firsthand (experiential) knowledge

- Correlating learning and enjoyment

- Unifying students around a common goal and shared experiences

Gaming and esports tap directly into this idea of experiential, hands-on learning and encourage learners to hone skills while learning traits such as fortitude, efficiency, empathy, dexterity, and innovativeness. When employing gaming in the classroom, it is important that we guide our students in conversations before and after the gaming takes place. Our discussions should help students make meaning of the game as it connects to our content. Further, we need to guide our students in critical discussion about how people, places, and ideas are fairly and unfairly represented in game play. As we see a rise in gaming with history and historical-fiction plot lines, our sensitivity toward representation must become amplified.

TWO

CHANGING PERCEPTIONS ABOUT ESPORTS

D espite its benefits, esports is sometimes dismissed by those who don't understand what it really is all about. Often the naysayers will bring up issues like violence in gaming or excessive screen time. It is important to be able to respond to stakeholders' concerns about these aspects of esports. To that end, here are responses to concerns you are likely to hear while pitching your esports team or discussing esports with community members.

VIOLENCE AND VIDEO GAMES

Some still posit that there is a relationship between real-life violence and violent video games. Yet studies have shown little to no correlation.

A decade-long study conducted by a group working with the University of Glasgow released in 2013 looked at the effects of television and video game use. The study included over 11,000 children across a massive cross-section of families. The findings showed that there was a positive correlation between conduct issues and watching television, videos, or DVDs for three hours or more each day. But the same results weren't found for video games.[1]

In 2019, researchers at the Oxford Internet Institute and the University of Oxford found no relationship between aggressive behavior in teenagers and the amount of time spent playing violent video games.[2] Their study used both subjective and objective data to measure teen aggression and violence in games. Earlier research had relied too heavily on self-reported data from teenagers, so this study was designed to use information from parents and guardians to help assess the level of aggressive behavior in their children.[3] "The idea that violent video games drive real-world aggression is a popular one, but it hasn't tested very well over time," said lead researcher Andrew Przybylski, director of research at the Oxford Internet Institute. "Despite interest in the topic by parents and policy makers, the research has not demonstrated that there is cause for concern."[4]

In February 2020, the American Psychological Association (APA) released an updated resolution to replace its August 2015 resolution that had been cited as evidence by many media outlets and policy makers that violent video games cause violence, including mass shootings.[5] In this updated resolution, the APA stated that there was insufficient scientific evidence to support a causal link between violent video games and violent behavior. "Violence is a complex social problem that likely stems from many factors that warrant attention from researchers, policymakers and the public," said APA president Dr. Sandra L. Shullman. "Attributing violence to video gaming is not scientifically sound and draws attention away from other factors, such as a history of violence, which we know from the research is a major predictor of future violence."[6]

Studies have also shown that while social media has a positive correlation with depression, video games do not.[7] Nevertheless, you can expect this myth to come up when pitching your esports team. In discussions with stakeholders while designing your club or team, have games of various ratings from Entertainment Software Ratings Board (ESRB) to fall back on, in case your preferred game is considered too violent for school.[8]

TOXIC GAMING CULTURE

Another frequently heard objection is that esports is mired in a toxic culture that has reared its ugly head in incidents like Gamergate (a misogynist attack on female gamers by a group of antifeminist gamers).[9] At the center of this attack was the developer of a game called *Depression Quest*. The developer's ex-boyfriend wrote a series of blog posts defaming her and falsely alleging inappropriate relationships that she had with others while they were dating. She became the victim of a horrible series of harassing events, including having her personal information shared. Horrible comments and accusations were posted, and she even received death threats. She felt forced to leave her home to protect her safety. This developer and other women were the targets of this movement and serve as a strong example of the ways that the parts of the gaming community have created an extremely toxic environment for underrepresented groups of gamers. While it's important to note that this harassment was conducted by a subsection of the gaming industry, the scars still run deep.

The only way to prevent events like this from occurring again is to provide proper support to our gamers and educate them on fundamental issues, such as empathy, sportsmanship, and digital citizenship. Rather than promote violence, esports is a perfect platform to help us work to prevent negative behaviors.

Esports, when supported and modeled in an appropriate manner, serves as a community builder that promotes both empathy for others and camaraderie. Esports is a powerful tool for promoting digital citizenship with students while providing a purpose and application for that skill beyond just checking off a lesson.[10] Additionally, playing into the interests of students, whether through esports or another pathway, encourages active participation in schools and a stronger overall student engagement. Esports serves as an inclusive opportunity to give voice and recognition to students who may not have otherwise chosen a role within the school community. Students who are not affiliated with esports are now able to see their peers in an entirely different light, which can result in admiration and respect for the esports athlete.

SCREEN TIME

It seems the research on screen time is similar to a lot of research about overindulgence: all things in moderation. A key point to make about this debate is that not all screen time is created equal. Passively consuming videos or watching a screen is completely different from becoming a producer of content—or a content creator, as the kids say. The skills that you develop as a content creator are applicable across a wide range of disciplines, and creating content helps kids develop valuable skills and a growth mindset that will likely help them be successful in other areas, away from the screen.

Your esports team will not be passive consumers. While esports clearly contain the competitive and recreational aspects of traditional sports, many people suggest that there isn't very much physically going on besides the hand-eye coordination needed to play games. But researchers have found that there may be more to esports than meets the eye.

Professor Ingo Froböse from the German Sport University Cologne became the first scientist to study the physical demands or strains that esports athletes face when competing.[11] His study involved conducting tests designed to determine the demands placed on the athletes' minds. This involved testing for the stress hormone cortisol. Froböse found that the cortisol levels produced by the competitors were equivalent to those produced by race-car drivers. In addition, the gamers were having to generate almost four hundred keyboard and mouse movements per minute during their competitions, which is four times what a normal person would be performing. When combined with the high degree of tactical understanding that is required for gamers and the high pulse rate produced during gaming, sometimes up to 160 to 180 beats per minute, which is what marathon runners and basketball players experience, it is clear that esports are more than passive screen watching. "In my opinion, esports are just as demanding as most other types of sports, if not more demanding," Froböse said.

Your esports team empowers students as creators of content because, as we discuss in more detail later in the book, being an esports competitor is just one of the different roles that a student can play on an esports team or club. Students are not just responsible for playing games, but also are responsible for hosting podcasts, editing video, and designing promotional flyers—in other words, creating content. And the content they create not only is of incredible value to the esports team or club, but it provides students with a portfolio of work that they can later use throughout their academic, and possibly even professional, careers. Be sure to highlight these various roles to stakeholders and the ways you'll be producing content to give them a broader sense of the scope of your esports initiative.

STUDENT PRIVACY

Stakeholders may ask how a student's privacy is being protected while playing a game or being featured on social media or during a stream. Have a student privacy policy and permission slip for stakeholders that outlines how, when, and if students' images and names will be used.

The IT department is often tasked with making sure software is used in a manner that conforms with laws like the Family Educational Rights and Privacy Act (FERPA) and Children's Online Privacy Protection Rule (COPPA). It is important that you are able to answer privacy questions before talking to the IT department. The IT professionals we've talked to suggest you do the following:

Read and have ready for IT the "use" policies associated with the games you want to play. Most commercial software, like video games, has something called an end-user license agreement (EULA) that outlines the contract you are entering into with the company by using their software. Games also have a terms of service (TOS) agreement. A TOS is similar to a EULA, but a TOS focuses on user behavior when using their software, including the expected age of the user. Most games will also have privacy policies that outline what, if any, personally identifiable information is being collected about their users. Whatever policies your game may have, it is important you are familiar with them and make them available to the IT department.

During installation, companies will often ask for personal information like name, phone number, and address. Before going to IT, you should research this—or even better install the game yourself—to determine what personal information is required from the user on setup. Determine if, while creating an account, a generic school email account can be used along with school information, like school address and phone number, instead of students' personal information. The best-case scenario is that you are able to make accounts for students without using any of their personal information.

If creating more opportunities for students isn't enough for a school or district to embrace esports, maybe the focus can be on the need to keep the young esports athletes safe. There is a gaming war brewing, with students as the primary targets, as hosts of startups are trying to win a piece of the esports-in-school pie. A startup, PlayVS, closed a $15 million round of funding to bring esports to high schools.[12] Undoubtedly, esports in education will need infrastructure and a governing body to be taken seriously. While colleges seem to have settled on the National Association of Collegiate Esports (NACE) for their governing body, NASEF has quickly become the go-to organization for the K–12 community (see Appendix for more about NASEF).

It is the duty of educators to make sure for-profit companies and startups vying for a piece of the control of esports in education keep the safety of our students as a priority. Because we don't know if educators and students had a voice at the table while these for-profit companies were creating their businesses plans, it is imperative that schools not only represent students but also protect them. Having educator and student voices heard is important. By embracing esports, we can provide a level of protection for students and hold companies accountable.

GENDER INEQUALITY

Esports can and should provide opportunities to participate for all students. In traditional school sports, clear lines are drawn in terms of participation based on both gender and athletic ability. And while esports still poses some challenges along these lines (rage issues, etc.), it also provides the greatest possibilities for us to attack gender inequality issues by providing a platform that allows all genders to participate and collaborate in ways other sports don't.

According to Elaine Chase, vice-president of Wizards of the Coast, "The single best way to attract women to your game and your events is to show women participating in your game and events. It can be such a blind spot when you're in the majority and used to seeing people like you everywhere; it just doesn't stand out. But when you're in a minority, seeing someone like you doing a thing, and being awesome at it, is powerful. It shows you that you belong and that you can succeed."[13] We need to be conscious of not only providing our female students with games that interest them, but we can also encourage more active participation by providing them with role models. The Leisure Economy Research Study by Playgroundz noted that "while women still make up half the gaming industry and are predicted to surpass the number of men by 2020, they make up only 30 percent of gamers on YouTube, 22 percent of esports team members, and 19.5 percent of gamers on Twitch. Women are playing, but they aren't willing to play for an audience."[14]

Luckily, there are many in the industry who are aware of the disparity and are making concerted efforts to empower females to take a more visible stance in esports. Wendy Lecot, head of strategic alliances and digital marketing innovation at HyperX, says, "Ensure that 50 percent of internships are for female talent. We encourage our female employees at HyperX to share what they do and why they love it. That could be on social or in special initiatives we have that help young women looking to enter a career in the gaming industry (via mentor chats)."[15] The more we empower our existing female gamers to be present and have a voice, the stronger role models there are for our aspiring female gamers who are looking for a mentor to inspire and guide them. Women in esports must band together to help one another as the industry continues to grow at an astronomical rate. As Esports Observer head of events Prinita Naidoo says, "For women who want to join the esports industry, stand your ground. Make your voice heard. Be confident and put yourself out there. That's something I'm definitely going to try to do more."[16]

Victoria Klimuk, the founder of the intramural *Overwatch* league at the University of Colorado Boulder, shared her story about getting into gaming and how she has observed improvement in gender diversity in the gaming community at her school over time. "Several years ago, there wasn't a space for women in gaming, for minorities in gaming," Klimuk said. "It felt like every time you got in a game, whether it was via text or via in-game voice communication, it just felt like a constant battle." This battle is not uncommon, but as Klimuk observed, gaming can become a more accepting, diverse environment if commitment is made to addressing these issues up front. "I've been seeing fewer and fewer of those moments for students on campus attending our events," Klimuk said. "We went from a 5 percent female attendance rate at some of our events to a third of them now."[17] Some studies have shown that as female participation increases, the levels of inequality in esports will continue to decrease.[18] Some of this can be attributed to the types of games that can be selected, which is, as we discuss later in this book, definitely an important part of the process of creating a club and league

Organizations out there have tried to address this issue. The Mischief League is a free, community-based, inclusive esports league for students in schools, libraries, and after-school clubs.[19] They rotate their games seasonally but choose them based on what will have a wide appeal to the greatest number of students. The Mischief League promotes digital-citizenship principles and looks to build communities for every level of gamer as well as provide an emphasis on the numerous career pathways available to students through esports.

TIPS FROM THE FIELD

AVOID THE *DIE HARD* EFFECT

Building an esports program that promotes diversity and gender equality is an important aspect that must be considered from the start of any esports initiative. But it also requires doing it in a mindful and thoughtful way. Just including student input on game selection doesn't necessarily ensure that you will wind up with a club or team that supports diversity. It can be very easy to fall into a trap that J Collins has called the *Die Hard* effect. As J puts it:

> If you start a film club at your school because you know that a lot of your students watch movies, and you go around and you

put up a bunch of posters and you say, "We're gonna have a *Die Hard* movie night. We're gonna show *Die Hard* with Bruce Willis and it's gonna be great!" Maybe ten students—all boys—show up and they're really excited to be there, but it's just ten students, right? And then you go the next week and you put up a poster that says, "Now we're gonna watch *Die Hard 2*," because that's what the ten students wanted to watch. And you get the same ten boys to show up. And then you watch *Die Hard 3*, and it's the same ten students, the same boys. And then you start saying, "Well, I guess girls don't like movies, right?"

I think that a lot of these leagues and a lot of other esports say, "Hey, your safest bet is to start with this game, start with these kids, and start doing it in this way." And funnily enough, all of the esports teams then start looking like each other, and they all start running into the same problems. And the problem—instead of a problem with the esports league—gets seen as a problem with *girls*. And people start saying, "Well, if only we could teach girls how to like *Die Hard*, then they would like movies." But there's a problem there.

DIVERSITY

In addition to female players being underrepresented, other groups do not participate as much in esports (either as players or operational contributors). Carrie Linden, the director of gaming for education at Progressive Learning Academy, shared how important it is to make the effort to include underrepresented populations in esports initiatives.

Many kids aren't seeing female gamers. Not enough to make it feel like they belong. And same thing with other minority groups. If you come into class and you're sitting in your esports class, and even a quarter of the people at the table are female or people of color or LGBTQ, you're doing massive amounts for them realizing that other people belong and that other people are there and that they're here. And they're my teammates, so now I've got this personal relationship with this person. We're communicating, we're collaborating, we're working on something together. It's not as far-fetched for them to accept somebody else now because, "Well, yeah, I've already got this person." That role already exists in their mind now and it has a place and it has purpose and it has relevance, so adding somebody else to that is easier. And I think that that's a great benefit to having gaming in education.

We have an opportunity and a responsibility to create safe spaces that encourage and foster inclusivity through esports, but the window to address the issue may be limited before it becomes a bigger challenge than it is now. Bo Ruberg, an assistant professor of digital games and interactive media in UCI's department of informatics, shared how important it is to make changes now, while esports is still a growing industry, before bad patterns and habits become embedded. "The longer something's been around, the harder it is to change the system," Ruberg said. "So I think because we're in a moment of shift, we can bring in those values, which are: everyone deserves to have a chance to be here. Everyone deserves to feel welcome, and we can bring them to esports."[20]

One of the best things about esports, however, is how accessible it is for students. Esports tends to draw students uninterested in traditional sports, including those who may have learning disabilities, physical handicaps, or are on the spectrum. Esports is popular with students of color, LGBT students, and less-affluent students as well. A Northwestern University study found, on average, black students play video games thirty minutes more per day than white students, while Latinx students play forty minutes more.[21] The Nielsen Company reports that 65 percent of all LGBT consumers play games of any type, slightly edging out heterosexual and cisgender players (63 percent).[22]

Researchers at AnyKey, an advocacy organization that supports diversity, inclusion, and equity in competitive gaming, produced the white paper *Diversity and Inclusion in Collegiate Esports.*[23] And while the paper focused on the collegiate level, there were clear applications for the high school level as well. Specifically, the paper included twelve recommendations to ensure that diversity and inclusion are at the forefront of school-based gaming initiatives. The recommendations are:

1. Perform a diversity audit and create a plan for inclusion.
2. Take preventative approaches before punitive ones.
3. Provide a code of conduct and enforce it.
4. Develop programs for diverse levels and forms of participation.
5. Encourage co-ed play.
6. Establish networks of support.
7. Use inclusive language and establish nondiscriminatory policies.
8. Offer meaningful diverse representation in media broadcasts.
9. Formulate holistic selection criteria for varsity teams.
10. Invest in a moderation infrastructure.
11. Provide formal training for bystanders and allies.
12. Incentivize and reward good social leadership.

We need to make sure the males who come through esports programs recognize their potential biases toward females and other genders as we help them learn how to advocate for equality in esports and beyond. Implementing these recommendations as part of any program you create will help with this, while also ensuring diversity in your program and promoting equity. Chances are you have an underserved population that is looking for a place to call home within your school. Esports can be that place. Once we can connect with these traditionally underserved students through the gaming they love, we can use it to create better learning outcomes for everyone.

EQUITY

Another concern that many critics of esports programs will bring up regarding diversity is the equity gap. Given that many esports teams play games on cutting-edge gaming machines and rock custom team jerseys, the argument is that in areas where funding is an issue, both at school and at home, esports would seem to be one more thing that will separate the haves from the have-nots. You may even think that bringing esports to your district requires spending thousands of dollars on flashy computers. That's a common misconception.

One question educators should ask themselves is whether equipment needs can be met using existing equipment in their school or district. Many schools have already invested in high-end computers for their STEM program, and a laptop computer or PC that can be used for STEM activities such as 3D design, video editing, or virtual reality can probably run your esports game of choice. If not, a great way to convince stakeholders to purchase compatible devices is to highlight their crossover use as both esports and STEM machines. And if you can't bring the computers to you, consider going to the equipment. Many businesses and colleges rent or donate space to scholastic esports teams. In New Jersey, colleges and LAN centers (which are private businesses designed to support networked multiplayer gaming) provide spaces for esports teams to practice. Find out what is nearby and see if they would be willing to work with your team.

Another potential solution to funding for a program is a bring-your-own-device (BYOD) approach. While somewhat limiting, depending on the types of systems students have access to at home, the grassroots approach of BYOD can get a program off the ground as other funding/accessibility options are explored. A classic example of this startup approach is the Garden State Esports league. More than two- thirds of the thirty teams are run using devices, such as Xbox One consoles, that students bring from home. Schools can fund programs through the PTA and even DonorsChoose. Because esports and STEM work so well together, many schools have received STEM grants to create their esports team. You don't need to spend a lot of money to start an esports team, but you must ensure equity is addressed in the development of your program.

CUT SCENE

CHALLENGE YOURSELF, CHALLENGE OTHERS

A sad truth is that there are many educators who may not view developing a program centered around diversity and equity as a priority. It is extremely important that, regardless of your background or ethnicity, you don't make that mistake. And while it's important for you to prioritize this in your program, it is equally important that you ensure that others are doing so as well. It is important for you to become an advocate on behalf of your students. And beyond your own efforts, make sure you find out how others are making efforts to ensure that esports are available to all. Bradford Harris, lead trainer for digital learning for the Aldine Independent School District in Houston, Texas, shared his experience:

> There are kids out there who want to get involved in esports, but they are going to tell you, "I don't have the money to do this. My parents don't have any money to do this."

> I am really big on making sure I expose as many black and brown children to esports as possible because it's not being seen. That's the reason I jumped into it. So every time I go somewhere, I start asking those hard questions. When I talk to companies at conferences, I'll ask, "What do you do for women and what do you do for people who look like me?" And I'm going to be honest. Those companies? They don't have an answer. They'll give me the generic answer. And I'm like, "That's not good enough." When I see many of these same people later at events like SXSW, they will pull me aside and say, "Thank you for asking me that question."

FUNDING

Finding funding for an esports program is one of the biggest challenges. If an esports program has not been budgeted for, there will likely be concerns about where the funding will come from. It is important to determine an appropriate budget that includes equipment like monitors, game licensing, potential accessories, like controllers, and environmental needs, such as seating. For many schools, this is made even more complicated by the need to work with approved vendors and purchase-order systems. While this may seem like a daunting task, it is achievable through careful planning and creative approaches.

It is important to plan for the unique funding issues that can arise with esports. For instance, if students will be playing on an Xbox, how will the school pay for the monthly subscription fee for Xbox Live, which is needed to play Xbox games online? Alternatively, some game licenses need to be purchased through Steam. A determination must be made as to whether students will compete on their own personal accounts or if the school will purchase and provide user accounts. An ideal approach that is fiscally beneficial is for schools to make accounts for students and purchase licenses for students using generic school email accounts. In using this model, the generic accounts/licenses can be passed from student to student, year after year. Generic accounts also better conform to privacy laws, which are critical for schools to follow.

A few examples of creative approaches to fund an esports program, as recommended by ByteSpeed, a hardware developer that serves as a catalyst in the esports education space, are:

- Utilize Career and Technical Education (CTE) funds—if the funder allows—for purchasing the equipment, as often it can be used for dual purposes. For example, esports PCs are capable of handling any type of CTE programs, like computer-aided design (CAD), video/photo editing, etc. Housing the machines in a shared space can allow for curricular-support uses during the school day and hosting esports after school hours.

- Local sponsorships are another popular means of obtaining funding. Consider onboarding several small businesses that donate small amounts instead of one big sponsor. It is helpful to draft a letter that can be used to communicate your needs as a program. In that letter, be sure to include information such as the student population, the vision and mission of your program, and a specific breakdown of where the donated funds will be spent. Local businesses are often interested in supporting school programs.

- Community use, in which schools rent out their facilities to generate revenue, is another means of potential funding. By charging general users a small hourly rate to use the computer equipment during off hours (when the esports team is not practicing or competing), you can utilize your equipment more often and get more value out of it, as well as engage community members in the purpose and mission of the program. This is also a helpful way to build understanding and respect for your program within the community. You may even want to consider hosting events as fundraisers, in which your athletes teach other community members how to play various games.

- Lastly, you can seek grants. ByteSpeed provides a specially curated list of STEM/EDU grants, many of which can be leveraged to source equipment that support esports. These grant resources can be found at https://www.bytespeed.com/resources/funding/. The Carl Perkins Grant, specifically for virtual reality funding, is the first link on the grants page. Schools are invited to directly copy that letter, add their info, and submit for a good chance at getting funding for VR equipment (which can also run esports games).

While it may seem like a burden to fund all the expenses that align with an esports program, if you break the work down into small, manageable pieces, it can be very achievable. Through creative funding sources, community fundraising (which is why it is critical to build understanding and respect in the community), and grants, funding for an esports program is attainable and realistic.

CUT SCENE ——————————————————————

FUNDING THROUGH TITLE I

Sandra Paul, director of IT and operations for the Township of Union Public Schools in New Jersey, worked with her leadership team to fund esports through a Title I grant.

As the director of grants and funding explained the application process and what they were looking to fund, she told me it would be great to have technology activities that would encourage students in an after-school program. During these discussions I made a case for esports being a beneficial program for the schools because it would help students in developing twenty-first-century skills and college and career readiness. I began researching how esports could have a learning and instructional focus, and I shared information with the district leadership on the value of having an esports program in the school. This information included how involvement in esports leagues boosts student engagement; drives learning outcomes, equity, and scholarships; and prepares students for the twenty-first century. Students develop critical thinking skills, learn to collaborate and work as a team, develop grit through overcoming failures, and learn to communicate with their team as well as other participants in the esports league.

Our next steps were to identify the advisor of the program, a location for it in the building, and the feasibility of running the program. In discussions with the advisor, we discussed what league the students would be involved in and what esports they would be playing (*Rocket League*). Then we had to find out if we would be an approved program for schoolwide Title I funding. Lo and behold, it was approved.

There was quickly a large interest developing at the high school, resulting in their first meeting having one hundred students sign up to be part of the program. Originally the students were interested in doing fundraising for the technology equipment for their program, but because of my experience with funding the middle school esports program, I thought to mention the program to the director of grants. We went through the same process for the high school.

Eventually, the high school program registered with the NFHS (National Federation of State High School Associations) and began following the PlayVS platform. The high school esports program will also be a part of the high school pathways program, where students will be choosing courses and following a designed pathway that will lead to college and career readiness. In the STEM pathway, students would have the choice of taking STEM electives. These electives include but are not limited to CAD (1, 2, 3, 4), Principles of Engineering, Intro to Computer Science, AP Computer Science, Introduction to Drone Theory and Design, Digital Arts, Forensic Science, etc. The Business Administration and Management (BAM) pathway includes electives such as Sports/Entertainment Management, Exploring Social and Digital Media, Public Speaking, Business Management, etc. With these pathways in mind, getting buy-in from the students, teachers, and administrators for this program in the high school has been focused on the future skills and knowledge our students will need for the twenty-first century.

Applying Title I funds for both of these programs provided opportunities for students in the district that they may not have had otherwise.

THREE

WORKING WITH STAKEHOLDERS

IDENTIFYING STAKEHOLDERS

One of the biggest challenges whenever you are starting a new project or program in your school is making sure you've communicated and coordinated effectively with all of the stakeholders in your district. It can be so easy to let our passion and excitement take over, but if you don't ensure that other important players in your school district are involved, your efforts could be doomed to failure. Communication is a critical component of building a program, but it shouldn't be limited to after your program is established. Creating buy-in is an absolute necessity in building your program.

TIPS FROM THE FIELD

ANSWER THE BIG QUESTIONS

Before approaching anyone in your school district about starting a program, it's important you are clear in your own mind about the reasons for and benefits of starting an esports program. Dennis Large, director of educational technology at the Riverside County Office of Education in Riverside, California, frames it this way:

> Ask yourself some questions: Why do you want to start an esports program? What are we expecting to get out of it? What are our goals as a school or as a district? And what sort of criteria are we going to set? Are we going to have set grade-point-average criteria, attendance criteria, behavior criteria, etc.? What are our social norms going to be? Then you want to get wider stakeholder input. Talk with teachers and administrators but also students and parents. Make sure that cabinet-level members of the district and board members are involved, because you don't want to start down this path and have some parents complain or something, and a board member hears about that and then suddenly things get shut down. That is never the way to get a program going, right?

ADMINISTRATION

We all know the importance of having the support of administration when starting any program. Esports is no exception. Where to start with this will often depend on your district's chain of command. More than likely, the building principal is the place to start, especially when you are trying to start a program within one school. The principal and their assistants run the day-to-day operations of the school and generally are the first level of approval you will need. After receiving support at the building level, it is important, as with any program, to gain district-level administrative approval (generally the superintendent, assistant superintendent, and the board of education).

We have made great strides already in bringing esports programs into schools. The general impression would be that a teacher or advisor or student group would initiate the process. In the early days of esports programs, it often seemed like an uphill battle. A lot of energy went into demonstrating why an esports program would bring value to the school and how the organization would get started (typically without funding). We have reached a point when it is not only the educator or students trying to get a program started—building- and district-level administrators as well as boards of education are starting to drive the effort to start esports programs. This shift is incredibly helpful in getting programs started, and even funded. Chris and Steve were asked to participate in the upcoming New Jersey School Boards Association Conference to promote esports through student competitions to be held at the event. Conferences like this bring the key stakeholders together and generally drive the trends, because members of boards of education attend. We have certainly turned a corner in terms of support from administrators.

Currently it seems as though most school districts are seeing esports as falling on the club/extracurricular activity spectrum. It is important that we get to a point where esports programs are valued on the same level as traditional sports programs. This can only happen by obtaining the support of administrators and other budget decision-makers. The level of commitment of student participants, advisors, and coaches is on par with athletic programs. Therefore, funding for esports programs should also be on the same level. Furthermore, there are many opportunities to integrate esports into the curriculum and provide opportunities for wide participation in CTE-related areas of study.

TEACHERS

As with any school activity, teachers are key stakeholders, whether it be as advisor, coach, or evangelist. Esports is at an interesting place. Many educators see the value and are interested in supporting the idea but may not have expertise in the area. This is a concern when it comes to coaching versus advising (discussed later). Many programs have started with a student group finding an educator who is willing to support a student-led initiative as an advisor. This is great, as it empowers students to take on leadership roles while having the necessary support of an educator. The educator is crucial in the process, because all clubs and activities need an adult figurehead. Students also need the educator to help support the formation of the club and as a liaison with the administration. Furthermore, when it comes to bringing esports content into the mainstream curriculum, it helps to have a strong educator advocate.

STUDENT SUPPORT SERVICES (SPECIAL ED, SOCIAL WORKERS, COUNSELORS)

One thing we have definitely come to understand is that esports serves a diverse group of students and learners. We often talk about the fact that many of the students who are drawn to esports might not otherwise have an affinity group or home-school connection. Many students with special needs find a safe place in their gaming community. Many students interested in esports are not involved in traditional sports or may not be as competitive in that arena, yet the playing field is level when it comes to esports. Esports also offers opportunities for participants interested in the gaming space, whether or not they choose to play competitively.

This is where the role of support services comes in. Many of these students need additional support and advocacy. It is so important that our esports programs are inclusive and welcoming to all interested students. It is important for support service personnel to understand the benefits and opportunities available through esports programs. They are in a unique position to help students find activities that are appropriate, and also serve as a liaison between the student and the advisor. Advisors need to understand specific student needs related to their Individualized Education Program (IEP), 504 Plan, and of course their emotional well-being.

Steve and Chris often speak of the fact that many of the students participating are on the autism spectrum or have a 504 Plan or IEP. They often meet with support services staff to better support the students. Steve has met many times with a counselor and student to determine if the club would be appropriate for the student, and to determine how they can work together to ensure that the student receives the support necessary.

IT DEPARTMENT

When starting an esports team, you'll spend a lot of time considering the needs and perspectives of stakeholders, like students, administrators, and the board of education. But a vital, yet often overlooked, stakeholder in your esports journey will be the IT department. The IT department is responsible for keeping a school's network safe, purchasing and implementing new technology, like the tech needed for your esports team, and ensuring compliance with safety and privacy laws for your district. Your IT department holds the keys to unlocking esports in your school. Before approval, and when it comes time for implementation, the IT department is a key stakeholder in your esports journey.

Over the last twenty years, the performance requirements and network demands of video games have increased dramatically. Most video games are now online only and are meant for a global audience. These demands mean that it falls to the IT department to get your esports team up and running on your school's equipment and network. Typically the IT department will have to provide the needed bandwidth, port availability, and firewall exceptions for your game to be played on your school's network, on top of installing any necessary software on school devices.

Schools with at least 1GB connections should have no problem running an esports team, especially because time of play is often after school, when there is less draw on network resources. Dedicated caching servers might also be required to implement and run games effectively on your network. There are dedicated services available that provide game caching for many of the more popular esports game producers/platforms, such as Steam, Blizzard, and Riot. Additionally, some networks that have specific restrictions on port access may require those ports to be opened or forwarded in order for the game to function. If this paragraph overwhelms you, don't worry. We spoke to many IT professionals to better understand what to expect when it comes time to discuss esports with the IT department.

The most important thing you should do before approaching your IT department is understand the concerns an IT department will commonly have about an esports team. By understanding these concerns, you can discuss them with all stakeholders so a plan can be put in place that works for everyone.

FACILITIES

An often overlooked stakeholder that is critically important to esports is the district facilities team. Be sure that the needs of the program are clearly presented and relationships are created so that matters related to facility use don't appear to be an afterthought. For example, if a new space is being created for esports, there will likely be power needs that extend beyond those of a normal classroom. Likewise, wired internet is crucial for online play, so wiring needs must be communicated between the facilities staff and the IT department.

School districts usually have a procedure for reserving space for events that fall outside of school hours. It is common for esports matches to fall outside of school and even regular after-school hours to accommodate different time zones. This makes it especially important to figure out the procedure and bring the responsible group into your stakeholder community. In many school districts, a facilities-request form must be submitted at least two weeks before any event.

PARENTS

Last but not least, one of the most important stakeholder groups to engage with is parents. And perhaps not surprisingly, this can be one of the most challenging groups to convince. At their core, parents' concerns stem from them wanting what is best for their child. If you manage to convince parents that there is value in an esports program, they can become powerful allies, supporting your vision and helping with everything from fundraising to advocating on behalf of your team or club.

So how do you begin to bring parents over? Organizations like NASEF do a number of webinars and provide a lot of information to schools targeted toward providing parents with information on the benefits of esports. Running an informational event for parents or even a school-based esports event is a great way to help them understand that esports is something bigger than just playing video games and is a wonderful ecosystem for their child to be involved in. Once they see the bigger picture, you may be surprised how quickly parents complete the journey from total skeptic to totally all in.

TIPS FROM THE FIELD

THE IMPORTANCE OF CONNECTING WITH PARENTS

Changing parent perceptions around esports and gaming in general can be a challenge. Planning how you will address parent concerns and foster their support should be at the forefront of your efforts to include stakeholders in the process. the payoff for the effort you put in can be huge. There could be literal tears of joy as a result of your work. Katie Salen Tekinbaş, professor in the Department of Informatics at UCI shared her experiences with parent involvement in esports programs:

> I do a lot of work in helping parents understand the value of gaming. NASEF has these events at the Santa Ana Esports arena. The teams are there, and the coaches and parents come. For many parents, it's the very first time they see their child in this kind of environment. I remember the first championship we went to, which was three years ago. Parents were crying because they understood something about their child that they hadn't understood before—that their kid wasn't the only one interested in this, that spending time with a game wasn't a negative thing. They saw how social it was. They saw the learning that was happening. They saw the community. The kids come out. Their schools come out and cheer. All these kinds of things. I think some parents can have a lot of very narrow mental models about the value of this kind of play.

CONVINCING STAKEHOLDERS

Once you have a vision for your esports team, data about your players, and support from mentors lined up, it is a good time to meet with stakeholders and formally discuss starting an esports program. Below are some talking points to help explain the value of esports in education to stakeholders.

Home-School Connection

Esports is likely to attract a population of students that are underserved by your school's extracurricular offerings. Students who come out for esports often don't have a home-school connection, meaning they might not be involved in other sports or clubs at school. Studies show that students who have a home-school connection have an increased academic performance. To that end, you may also want to consider adding behavior, attendance, and grade eligibility requirements to strengthen this home-school connection. The improved academic performance that comes from being involved in school activities combined with the addition of traditional eligibility requirements is a strong one-two punch of a value proposition.

CUT SCENE

MAKING FAMILY CONNECTIONS

Some of the best stories we've heard about the power of esports center around students and families who previously felt very little connection to their schools but found a bond through esports. Dennis Large shared this story:

> Within our own county office, we run what we call alternative-ed programs for kids who have been expelled from the local school districts. These programs serve as a sort of a last resort for them. We decided to take one of our schools and start an esports program there. Those kids were so excited. They were so happy, especially when we told them, "Not only are you gonna have a club and a team, but we're building a league, and you get to participate in a tournament against other schools in the surrounding districts."

> The next day, the advisor called me and said that one of the kids went home and told his parents about it, and the mom called the school and said, "Can his dad and I go to a tournament?" I said, "Yeah, of course!" They said, "Oh, thank you. Also, can others come? My sister, his aunt, lives in Sacramento. She wants to fly down to see him play." And when I first heard that, I thought, "Well, that seems weird."
>
> But then I thought about it more: Sometimes we're dealing with kids who have not had successes in schools before, kids who have not been invested in something school-related before. And here are some families who are now excited about what their kid is excited about at school. So of course they want to go and see this, to be part of it. They wanna see their kids doing something they're passionate about, especially when the school is honoring and respecting it.

Social/Emotional Development

While esports may be a scholarship opportunity for some, the social/emotional benefit can impact all your players. Providing students with mentorship, modeling, and guidance on how to have a positive online experience is a benefit to your students and the online gaming community. Further, through your esports team, students may find a new friend group and sense of belonging, both of which lead to better learning outcomes for students. Jonah, a student at Rutgers University and member of Rutgers Esports, offered this observation:

> Scrimmaging against other schools/teams can build a healthy relationship between teams and schools. An example would be from my time at Rutgers. Rutgers and New Jersey Institute of Technology (NJIT). *Overwatch* players who often play and scrimmage against one another sometimes hang out online or even in person. It was the same for Rutgers and University of Toronto players (esports is able to

bridge national gaps).International students at Rutgers were able to find a place in our esports community, too, since the game itself does not change from country to country. This allowed international students to successfully develop social bonds with domestic students through playing and practicing together.

Even though Jonah is speaking from his experience at the college level, it is easy to imagine relationships between players from different schools growing through competitions, as well as international and ESL students finding a place on your esports team.

Career Exposure

According to popular esports game developer Blizzard, there is an increasing number of career opportunities in the esports industry.[1] Many of these are behind-the-scenes jobs that make a professional gamer's career possible. Use your esports team to introduce students to different professions and career paths. Esports teams have accountants, broadcasters, technicians, marketeers, and many other employees working for them. A strong educational esports program will find ways to incorporate students in roles other than players so they can be exposed to different career possibilities in the fastest-growing industry in the world. The best esports programs in education are made up of both players and support roles.

TIPS FROM THE FIELD

BEYOND PROFESSIONAL GAMING

Many esports players fantasize about becoming professional gamers in very much the same way that traditional athletes dream of going pro. There are an incredible number of opportunities for students to participate in your esports program beyond the games themselves that can lead to positive outcomes ranging from college scholarships

---

to professional careers. Highlighting these opportunities to students early on is critical, as it allows for students to build skill sets that can benefit them greatly as they embark on their academic and professional career paths. As Kevin Brown from NASEF puts it:

> The real message we're putting out now is not that this is a path to pro, it's path through pro. Some kids, just like the ones who are really good on the green or really good on the blacktop, that's the 0.005 percent that go on to play in the NBA, in the NFL, in the NHL, become Olympians—rarefied air. So it is with esports. It's a possibility if you love it, if you chase it, if you get good, then go for that, absolutely—but have a backup plan. Go to school. Realize that esports of all the sports that are out there have a really tight margin. You shoot up the rankings and you go for about ten to fifteen months, you drop down, you go away. You don't get endorsement deals. Nobody calls you again once you've been lapsed, so you better have a plan.
>
> With hockey, you don't have to be an NHL player, you just have to love hockey. So whether or not you're Wayne Gretzky, you can still get a job in hockey. Marketing it, talking about it, broadcasting, color commentating. All those things you can still do to touch the thing you love, and you know what? It pays you. So we want kids to take that next step. College is part of it. Pro might be, honestly, not for everybody, but you can still be in the world and have great things happen.

The esports ecosystem consists of many skills. It is important for esports programs to acknowledge the variety of opportunities to support students in areas that expand far beyond the player. The graphic provided by NASEF provides a great overview of the many ancillary roles that exist within the realm of esports.

Anderson, Tsaasan, Reitman, Lee, Wu, Steele, Turner & Steinkuehler (2018)

These skills represent opportunities for many students to get involved in esports, even if they are not highly competitive or skilled game players. Our experience in esports has definitely shown this to be true. We've seen students who were avid spectators get involved in strategy and coaching, including watching and analyzing film (game replays) to support their team. Likewise, many schools have developed (or enhanced existing) video production and editing programs by providing opportunities for students to broadcast and announce matches, create post-production videos, and so much more.

Entrepreneurship opportunities in web design, business development, marketing, and event organization create pathways for students to participate in esports. This covers areas like fundraising, branding, etc. For example, Chris is a big proponent of entrepreneurship in education, and one of the student-run businesses he helped develop was an event company in which students ran *Fortnite* tournaments at a local pizzeria. Efforts like this have proven to be very effective. Other school fundraising events include LAN parties, open tournaments, jersey sales, and of course, bake sales!

Organizers work behind the scenes to make matches possible. They oversee the scheduling process by reaching out to opposing teams to schedule matches. Organizers also work with the school administration on securing spaces for competitions. Organizers can also market esports events by promoting them digitally on social media and creating flyers to hang around the school. Finally, organizers set up the equipment, troubleshoot issues, and make sure the audience has everything they need to enjoy the event.

Strategists are an underutilized department of the esports team. They can track team performance in key areas to show improvement over time, use this data to identify team weaknesses, and help develop a practice plan. Strategists can scout opponents, identify weakness, and help prepare a game plan for upcoming matches. The day of a match, strategists can help coaches and even feed data and statistics to the broadcasters to use in commentary. And those are just some of the ways strategists can contribute to an esports team.

Many of our students watch streamers and YouTube creators all the time. These have become their go-to celebrities. The thought of becoming a creator is very appealing to our students, and this is a big aspect of esports. Students can participate in video production and editing, graphic design, and animation, as well as livestreaming and shoutcasting. It is important that our esports programs provide these options. Students can learn valuable skills that are meaningful to them while contributing to the esports program. This is a great way for students who may not be star players to get involved and take center stage.

Students involved in esports programs can learn great IT skills. When we empower students in all aspects of programs, we put a lot of the learning in their hands. Students can actively learn about gaming hardware and infrastructure needs (internet bandwidth, etc.), which includes everything from determining the viability of playing on a hard-wired versus wireless network to understanding system and network requirements to run games. It is great when students are involved in determining and pitching the team needs and developing a solid plan to ensure that their program can run on the school technology. Some schools embrace this as a way to teach students how to build their own computers in order to learn valuable skills while saving some money.

CUT SCENE

NOT JUST PLAYING GAMES

Chris Vocelka, a highly ranked *Rocket League* player who goes by the gamer tag "Topher Jaims," spent eight years as an instructor at Bellevue University in Nebraska before moving to Massachusetts to become Uptime Esports's broadcast coordinator. In that role, he trains kids in learning the production side of esports. He shared this story:

> I moved out here to Massachusetts this past August, and my mom and stepdad, Mike, tell people, "Oh, Chris moved out there to play video games." And I'll scream at them up and down, "I'm not playing video games! I'm an IT specialist/social media professional, and I'm hardcore busy."
>
> My little brother just visited me. He is nineteen years old, going to a community college, and isn't really sure what he wants to do in the future. I showed him the center where I work, and he was like, "Oh, this is amazing!" He loves video games. And I asked him, "Are you interested in learning? Because I'm gonna show you a bunch of stuff."
>
> He has one of those shy personalities. So we had a *Fortnite* tournament one Saturday, heavy, in-depth. We tried to take in a ton of audio and video connections for our broadcast, and so it was no surprise that the system stopped working or didn't work half the time. And my little brother took the broadcast control and . . . he just took it over. He's like, "All right, we're gonna use this feed, we're gonna use this web camera,

and we're gonna do this, we're gonna do that." He's just the maestro of everything. I'm running around making sure everything works while I'm casting on a microphone. I go up to him, I'm like, "Are you good?" He's pushing buttons. "Yeah, I'm good." And I said, "Maybe we got a new career here." When I dropped him off at the airport, I looked him straight in the eye. I said, "You tell Mom and Mike I'm not just playing video games. You now know firsthand that I'm not just sitting here playing video games."

School-College Pipeline

Many colleges have esports programs and some have even started to offer scholarships. Even if a student doesn't earn a scholarship, an esports team that has partnered with high schools, colleges, and universities will have created a pipeline for students interested in esports that can keep them involved in esports from middle school through high school and into college. The best esports programs will have partnerships with multiple esports programs and leverage those relationships in a way that helps students see what the next level looks like and how they can get there.

CUT SCENE

A PEEK INTO COLLEGE RECRUITING

Many people don't realize that the college recruiting process for esports athletes very much mirrors the process for other sports, like basketball and football. Potential recruits are identified and scouted early in their high school careers. But the recruiting and scholarship opportunities don't just stop with the gamers. There are a number of ways for students to earn esports scholarships to colleges, both playing the games and serving in other capacities. And as esports continues to grow, so will the number of scholarships and career opportunities for students to pursue. Here's Dr. Chris "Doc" Haskell, professor and head coach of esports for Boise State University:

> We're looking for the next generation of broadcasters. We're thinking about the people who are gonna come in and be our storytellers, and so we're looking for opportunities to offer scholarships in that way. We already offer scholarships on the production side of broadcasting. And, again, with a space like that, we do a ton of broadcasting. And our broadcast studio specifically for esports would rival a lot of local news stations. And we probably put out more content than a lot of small-town local news stations, the idea being that we're giving these students an opportunity to be really successful. This year, we'll give a small scholarship to a player who is also a journalism major, and part of that scholarship is the expectation of weekly articles on different topics that publish directly to our website, but also straight to the Boise State website.

We've explored some ways to lay the groundwork for getting a program off the ground in your school or district. Getting buy-in from the various stakeholders in your community is a critical part of the process. And now that we've looked at the variety of roles that students can take part in through an esports program, you have the knowledge you'll need to move forward. In the next chapter, we will take a look at how you can begin to design or enhance your own program.

— FOUR —

DESIGNING AN
ESPORTS PROGRAM

WHICH MODEL IS RIGHT
FOR YOUR SCHOOL?

There are many things to consider when launching an esports program. For example, will the program serve as a club or team or be taught from the classroom through an esports-themed curriculum? Be offered during the school day or as an extracurricular? Have a coach or advisor? All of these questions and more will be explored in this chapter.

Esports will look different in every school. Teams will practice before school, during lunch and recess, or after school. Some programs will practice every day; some will practice once or twice a week. Some esports programs will focus on one game. Some will play multiple games. Some programs will look like a more casual gaming club, and some will be a competitive varsity program. You'll want to understand all the options you have for your esports team, but ultimately it should operate in a way that is best for your players.

Team

Many people who are invested in the idea of esports in schools believe that it should be treated like a varsity sport. There has been debate as to whether it should be modeled after traditional sports or programs such as forensics or robotics. Most up-and-coming esports programs are leaning toward traditional sports, which brings up the question as to whether it should be governed by sports associations and fall under the athletic director in terms of school administration, funding, and organization. Competitive gaming is similar to traditional sports when it comes to high-level performance in that it requires the same level of commitment to practice. Preparing an esports team for competition is right in line with the demands of traditional sports. As in traditional sports, students must maintain their grades and attendance in addition to dedication to the team. Varsity esports programs look very much like traditional sports programs. Treating esports programs on par with varsity programs requires the same commitment from the school in terms of funding, transportation, and overall support of the program.

As we've discussed, not every esports participant needs to be a gamer. Similar to how traditional football programs have equipment managers, statisticians, announcers, and more, innovative esports programs are finding ways to include non-gamer students by building true teams with behind-the-scenes roles. Esports teams have found homes for students interested in casting—the art of commentating on esports matches. There are also opportunities for students to run teams' social media accounts and live streams. Students can help set up matches, equipment, and marketing plans. Like the backstage crew of a school's theater program, lots of secondary roles can be filled by students on an esports team. These managing and technical roles help students learn real-world skills in career paths they may be interested in, while also fostering the same teamwork and communication skills esports players are developing.

Club

It may take time to get your esports program on a level with varsity sports, or you may want to bring esports to your school more casually. The club model can look very different from the traditional sports/varsity model. Many schools want to provide an affinity space for kids interested in gaming, which could lead to a spin-off involving competition for kids within the club, or even moving to the next level and creating a true esports team.

There is definitely a place for casual gaming in schools, and this model is often seen as a point of entry in elementary and middle schools. An esports team as a video game club would likely not limit the number of students who can join and would likely have a casual approach to competition. Students might come together and compete against each other, in-house, for fun rather than taking on teams from other schools. There wouldn't be tryouts or cuts, and practice would not be mandatory.

Gaming clubs provide community for like-minded kids, an authentic space to teach digital citizenship and responsibility, as well as a place to support SEL and soft skills in other ways. They are also a great environment to test the waters for competitive gaming through in-house tournaments, ladders, and leagues. When students are given the chance to play competitively against other schools, they gain a better understanding of the entire esports ecosystem and the excitement and opportunities it provides.

It is worth noting that there is a definite distinction between a true esports program (with a strong focus on modeling a schedule of practice and matches after varsity sports programs) and a club, which emphasizes providing a casual space for those interested in playing games. Both models, club and team, have value, and there is room for both to coexist and for one to morph into the other. You'll have to feel out what is right for you and your district—perhaps even both models. For example, Rutgers University holds both general-interest meetings designed for the student body and a separate competitive-interest meeting, where students who are looking for a more structured, serious esports experience can find teammates and enter collegiate tournaments against other colleges.

CUT SCENE

A TALE OF TWO ESPORTS APPROACHES

Steve has had the good fortune to work in a district where he has been able to build esports programs at both the middle and high school levels. However, that didn't necessarily mean that each one required the same approach:

> At William Annin Middle School, after-school programs are pay to play, meaning that clubs are only run if they can support themselves financially, based on registration. When it came time to consider an esports team or club, it made sense to start with a club for a number of reasons. In our case, it was

important to ensure that we met the participation requirements to run the club. However that was only a small part of
the decision. We were looking to create an inclusive environment for any student interested in gaming. The goal was to
have competitive gaming grow out of this, and it did.

Our game club is still thriving, and it creates a very positive
social environment for like-minded kids. It is important that our
kids have these spaces when we think about SEL, relationship
building, and feeling like a valued part of a community. It must
be acknowledged, however, that this is very different from a
competitive esports team. The club is much more casual, and
I believe it made the shift for some kids to esports, with greater
expectations around practice and commitment, more difficult.
On the other hand, when we started our program at Ridge
High School, we marketed it as a competitive esports program
from the beginning. It is run like a traditional sport. Participants
are expected to be fully committed to the practice schedule.
Students work with qualified coaches and cover everything
from traditional practice, drills, reviewing video, and spending
a lot of time discussing strategy and in-game communication skills.

Classroom

Several organizations have released curricula related to esports. NASEF
has developed four distinct curricular tracks, and they are all freely
available online.[1] Their English language arts curriculum is a four-year
course of study that connects esports with English language arts (ELA)
content standards. The coursework is aligned to the Next Generation
Science Standards (NGSS), the International Society for Technology in
Education (ISTE) standards, English Language Arts Common Core State
Standards (CCSS), and SEL.

NASEF has also developed a curriculum for career and technical education (CTE) for students in grades eight through twelve. The gaming industry is a multibillion dollar a year industry with many career opportunities. It only makes sense to help support students in developing the skills sought after in the field. NASEF is also developing curricula for middle school, as well as curricula geared toward out-of-school time to give students the chance to take advantage of the number of diverse opportunities that esports offers.

TIPS FROM THE FIELD

DIFFERENTIATE ESPORTS AND GAME-BASED LEARNING

You may be familiar with the term "game-based learning." Since esports involves games, is it the same thing? Yes and no. While you can embed aspects of gaming into your instruction and learning through esports, that does not make esports the same thing as game-based learning. Jonathan Spike, coordinator of instructional technology integration services at the University of Wisconsin-Whitewater, elaborates:

A lot of times with game-based learning, we're very purposeful, using aspects like parts of a game, or targeting certain types of games—whether it's a serious game or an educational game—and we're trying to use them strategically in the skills we want to develop. Whereas with esports, you're really trying to home in and master and practice specific skills to be really good at a particular game. You're trying to master your skills at, say, *Rocket League*, or *Rainbow Six*, or *League of Legends*. Whereas with game-based learning, we're trying to take those aspects of a game and really tie them to specific skills. With game-based learning, we're trying to reappropriate games to fulfill our needs in our curriculum.

Another alternative is the Gaming Concepts curriculum, created by Dr. Kristy Custer and Michael Russell, two educators in Kansas, in partnership with the High School Esports League.[2] The curriculum is intended to be delivered as a semester-long course that includes computer maintenance, digital citizenship, shoutcasting, setting up an esports team in school, and much more. Their curriculum is featured in the hour-long online course Build a School to Career Pipeline with Esports and Gaming Concepts on the Microsoft Educator Center.[3]

Another often overlooked aspect of an esports team is when the team meets. Esports teams often meet after school, while an esports team that has an academic curriculum tied to it likely meets during class. Some schools have had success with running their team during lunch, recess, or during a class like study hall. By having your team practice at times other than after school, you increase the likelihood of students attending, since they then can pursue more traditional sports, clubs, or part-time jobs after school. If you aren't getting the turnout you'd like for your esports team, consider moving your team's practice to one of these off-peak times.

Coach versus Advisor

Esports in education is at an interesting point. Many educators did not have opportunities in esports growing up so they have not gone up through the system like a coach of a traditional sport may have. This will certainly change over time, but at the present, it requires us to consider creative approaches to coaching.

As the teacher in charge of an esports team, you will probably have one of two roles: coach or advisor. As the coach of the esports team, you will be responsible for leading or helping lead day-to-day practices. While knowing how to play the game your esports team plays is helpful, it is not necessary to be great at the game to be a great coach. The National Association of Esports Coaches and Directors (NAECAD) (http://www.naecad.org) is a professional organization that formed in 2019 and offers professional development, including online certification, clinics, and conferences to support programs and connect coaches and directors.

Chris, who coaches the FH Knights, helps his team learn to play *Rocket League* despite having never played the game until starting the esports team. He watched tutorial videos, talked to high-level players, and recruited students from Rutgers University to help educate him on playing *Rocket League*. He feels confident coaching the team because he has a traditional sports coaching background. The way you coach esports is not much different from the way you coach traditional sports.

If you feel you don't have the game sense or the coaching background to lead the team, you may want to take on the role of advisor. The job of an advisor is to organize the team, find competitions, and most importantly, find a coach. A coach can be a student on the esports team, a student from a local college, or even virtual, a popular option for scholastic esports teams. Virtual coaching organizations like NASEF's free Connected Coaches initiative can provide you with the coaching you need to take your game to the next level. This program is provided as a partnership between NASEF and Connected Camps (connectedcamps.com).

TIPS FROM THE FIELD

DIVE RIGHT IN

With so many different ways to bring esports into a school or district, the various options could easily overwhelm anyone. So how does one know where to begin? Kimberly Lane Clark, director of blended learning for the Lancaster Independent School District in Texas, shared that the best advice she could offer in starting to build your esports program is to visit different esports arenas and student competitions to talk to as many people involved in the sport as possible:

Look at how the events are set up, talk to teachers, talk to districts that already have invested in it. Just put your boots on the ground and make sure you do your research first.

BEGINNING STEPS

While every educator's path to starting an esports team will be different, we will all likely encounter similar barriers to entry. Below are some of the most common steps you'll need to take.

Choosing the Game

You need three main things to start your esports team: stakeholder input and permission, equipment, and players. These three things usually depend on what game(s) you plan to play. The game you play determines who will come out for your team, what equipment you will need, and whether you can get stakeholder permission. That is why it is best to start an esports team by first planning what game(s) you'll play. To that end, one of the most important things to consider when picking games is the rating.

The Entertainment Software Rating Board (ESRB) ratings are E for Everyone, T for Teen (13+), and M for Mature (17+). If your school district's esports program is exclusively high school, you may be able to select a game that is T, based on age. In a school district where younger students may be players or spectators, like middle school, an E game is age appropriate. Games rated M would probably be the most controversial choice for your school's esports team.

LIST OF POPULAR ESPORTS GAMES BY ESRB RATING[4]

Everyone	Teen (13+)	Mature (17+)
FIFA	Apex Legends	CS: GO
Madden NFL	Dota 2	Call of Duty
Mario Kart	Fortnite	Dota Underlords
Minecraft	Hearthstone	Rainbow Six
Rocket League	Heroes of the Storm	Vainglory
Super Smash Bros.	League of Legends	
	Overwatch	
	Paladins	
	Smite	
	StarCraft II	
	Valorant	

When picking a game, consider whether you want students working together or playing on their own. Just as in traditional sports, in esports, football, basketball, and baseball are team sports, while wrestling, gymnastics, and boxing are individual sports. Consider, too, the intent of your program. Individual player games like *Hearthstone* offer deep strategy and logic-based critical thinking, while a team sport like *Rocket League* will produce more peer collaboration and communication. Identify your goals and select a game that will enable you to achieve them. For example, if your goal is collaboration and communication, consider team-based games.

It is important to note that the ESRB does not rate interactions for online gameplay. This means that while a game may be rated T, the interactions students have with others online is not and cannot be rated. *League of Legends*, for example, is a teen-rated game but is widely considered to have one of the most toxic player bases in esports; in other words, while the game itself is acceptable for teens, students often come across inappropriate content while playing online. Have a plan for how you will manage online student interactions with others outside your school ecosystem.

Finding and Managing Equipment

While there is a competitive esports scene for consoles with games like *FIFA, Madden,* and *Super Smash Bros.*, the esports scene is dominated by PC gaming. Serious esports programs that are looking to take on other schools will want to go the PC route. A lot of clubs start out on consoles as a point of entry, but usually with the goal of eventually transitioning to PC gaming.

The major hitch to keep in mind is the difficulty of competitive play on consoles with people who are not in the same room. Additionally, console gaming allows only a limited number of people to play. *FIFA, Madden,* and *Smash Bros.* are typically one-on-one (1v1), whereas PC games like *Rocket League* (3v3), *Overwatch* (6v6), and *League of Legends* (5v5) will allow you to get more kids playing at the same time.

PC Gaming	
Pros	**Cons**
Standard for competitive esports	More expensive than consoles
Thriving communities	Harder to find and get approved at the district level
No monthly fee to play games online	
Can be used for other educational activities	
New parts can be added to extend life	

Console Gaming	
Pros	**Cons**
Not as expensive as PCs	Not as popular or competitive as PC-based esports
Easier to start an esports team	Can't be used for purposes other than esports
	May have a monthly subscription fee to play online
	Reach end-of-life faster

Equipment depends on the game(s) that you are playing and the goals of your program. Some clubs start with having students bring in their own devices. A BYOD policy for both PC and console gaming is a great way to start an esports pilot program and/or develop interest in the sport. Most esports teams that play console-based games usually use BYOD to run their team.

Most esports games are played on a PC. As your esports program becomes larger and more competitive, you'll need to look into PCs with dedicated graphics cards. Start investigating funding early in the creation process, as it is usually the biggest barrier to entry for a school. Some schools make room in their school budget, others will do some type of fundraising. A lot of schools look toward sponsorship from big manufacturers or the local community. These are not as common as people would like to believe and usually require work on the school's part to demonstrate the return on investment (ROI) for the potential business sponsor.

The most effective way to fund a space like this is to make it multifunctional. Most schools have some kind of on-campus STEM presence. The graphics cards in gaming machines (plus their other specifications) can handle most of the applications that a STEM program would require. The gaming cards are specifically designed to run VR, which some schools are exploring. Successful schools have presented curricular use for this equipment during the day and shown the value of supporting an esports program after school.

Although schools might be tempted to purchase laptops because they are highly mobile and seem to have the correct specifications for esports and beyond, they generally do not have the cooling capacity to support extended gaming sessions. The way that these machines would be used (constantly plugged in and mobile) also hurt their longevity. Growing in popularity, small form factor (SFF) PCs do a better job keeping cool then their laptop counterparts. These SFF PCs can be put in a cart with monitors to provide a robust mobile solution. SFF PCs' price point is often lower than a laptop of comparable quality, providing more bang for your buck. Some programs have built their own PCs as part of the club—another cost-saving measure and a great learning experience for the students.

Minimum requirements are important to consider in shopping for a laptop or PC. As with traditional sports you need certain equipment to compete. Soccer, football, and baseball all require cleats to compete. Some say you need brand-name gear to compete at an elite level, some say you don't. We want to establish what "cleats" are when it comes to equipment for esports and leave the decision up to you.

Something else to remember about performance: while most people play games at settings that push their machines to the limit, almost all esports games have the option to turn down the graphics settings for better performance. If teams intend to run their games in this performance mode, like most pros do, they can likely get away with a less powerful PC. Always check the minimum requirements to run a game and see how your equipment compares.

Many people believe that having an expensive gaming keyboard, mouse, or headset makes a difference in performance. This isn't the case. A lot of the features that make name-brand peripherals attractive can be found on much less-expensive peripherals, and they're just as good. Either way, when it comes to peripherals, the best practice is to have kids bring their own peripherals. Getting used to the setup and feel of peripherals is an important part of becoming a better player. Let players use their own peripherals for practice and matches.

A gaming computer or console will need software updates, and the games themselves are constantly patched, so they will need to be updated before students can play. This means that your practices could be delayed by both a system update and a game update, especially if your team practices infrequently. Esports teams should check for updates hours before practice or matches so that any update has time to download and install.

When selecting a gaming platform, take into consideration recurring costs of online subscriptions for online play. If your school chooses Xbox and you have six Xbox consoles for students, then you will need six Xbox Live subscriptions, which can be purchased in monthly, quarterly, or yearly terms. While you could choose for students to log in to their personal Xbox Live accounts, removing this cost from the school, you may prefer that your school pay for and maintain the subscriptions so that you can invite a player who does not regularly use that platform. Most computer-based games don't come with this monthly cost but will cost more upfront, because gaming PCs are more expensive than consoles like Xbox or PlayStation. A final consideration is that consoles generally fall out of use when the next generation of consoles come out, whereas PCs can be upgraded to stay usable over time.

IT Considerations

Aside from purchasing and installing the game, you also have to consider the location where gaming will occur. Is there already an established network, preferably an access point, in the area? If not, IT will likely have to install the necessary equipment so you have the bandwidth needed not to lag while playing. This can add to the time and cost of getting a team up and running, so make sure you scout multiple locations. Areas where a lot of students congregate, like the library, tend to have the best network infrastructure.

Many esports teams are interested in streaming their matches to a platform like Twitch. Just as you should do your homework about the game you want to play, you should do your homework about streaming. Talk to stakeholders about streaming and the rules you will implement around it, and make sure to include these expectations in your permission slip for parents and your conduct policy for students.

You may need to do some convincing when working with the IT department. One of the most productive ways to prepare to talk to IT is to reach out to existing esports programs, preferably ones playing the game(s) you plan to play, and ask questions. Bonus points if the district is closer to yours. Precedent is the best thing you can have when trying to convince IT staff (all stakeholders, really). If you can point IT to multiple districts, the closer the better, that have an esports team and speak to how they handle IT concerns, you are much more likely to convince a hesitant IT department. Ask districts with esports teams if they are willing to have their IT department talk to your IT department to help allay concerns, work through implementation details, and share best practices.

Last, and maybe most importantly, understand that getting an esports team up and running takes time. Give IT enough time to research, test, and implement everything you need to succeed. Remember: the best way to cut down on the time and energy it takes IT to get your team up and running is to do your homework and come prepared with a plan of action that addresses the most common concerns your IT department may have. The IT staff will thank you!

Holding an Interest Meeting

An interest meeting with students is a significant step in launching an esports team. You can hold an interest meeting after finding equipment and getting a game approved, but it is probably more valuable to hold an interest meeting before then. The data you will gather at an interest meeting will help inform what type of game(s) students want to play and thus what equipment you might need.

During the interest meeting, collect data on what games students want to play and when they would be available for practice. It is also a good idea to collect demographic data like gender, grade, age, and current extracurricular-activity involvement. This data will be valuable when you pitch your esports team to stakeholders.

Further, the interest meeting is the perfect time to make the team rules and expectations clear. Students should know how esports is different from playing games at home, so you will want to set the tone for your esports team and how it will be run from the start. Will practice be mandatory? Will eligibility have a grade and behavior component? How will poor behavior and disrespect, often called BM (bad manners) or "being toxic," be handled? Will you have a substance-abuse policy like most varsity sports? If you're not a coach, ask a coach what they cover at their interest meeting and the policies they have in place for their players. By modeling the way traditional sports handle these issues, esports in education gains legitimacy as a "real sport."

Last, remember to lay out your vision for the team, your "nonnegotiables," while also making sure to allow students to share their vision, too. Building the rules and creating the culture of your esports teams with student voice at the interest meeting and beyond will lead to a much stronger esports program.

RUNNING A SUCCESSFUL ESPORTS PROGRAM

Growing the Program

The first step in growing a program is to reach out to all students and let them know it is a low-risk environment. Students who are casual gamers may be unsure whether they are good enough to join, and it is very important to reassure them that it's just for fun. Make a special effort to reach students whom many would not expect to be gamers. The key to reaching these students is providing them with a fun social experience. Events like a *Mario Kart* event, a *Just Dance* competition, or a *Wii Sports* night will attract students who would not come to a *League of Legends* tryout. This process should hopefully increase the diversity on the team, as students who felt like they "didn't belong" before will now know they're welcome and that they can compete just as well as anyone else.

Once the students feel accepted and know they won't be mocked (because we've created a nontoxic environment), they'll keep coming back and try more games. Eventually, you can encourage them to play a match of your esports team's favorite games. Make sure, however, that the teams are balanced. It does no one any good to just crush new players on their first try. This is also an opportunity for the competitive esports players to use leadership skills to coach and assist new players. It is vital to instruct them first on how to use simplistic language and directions as they coach so as to not intimidate the new players.

Keep in mind that learning a new competitive game is challenging. It will take a lot of effort and failure to eventually succeed. Give constructive criticism, but be sure to focus more on the positives and what a new player did well. Over time, the new players will gain experience and may want to try out for the esports teams. This is great for all involved because the player pool at the school will be larger, which generally leads to higher quality teams.

TIPS FROM THE FIELD

USE A GAMING CLUB AS A BUILDING GROUND

John Robertson, director of esports at Tipton High School, helped start the first Indiana esports league for high schools.[5] John shared his experience with running his esports team as a club:

> By casually talking to students, you'll quickly realize that many of them play video games and enjoy it but don't try competing on a higher level. This is especially true for demographics that are typically underrepresented in gaming. By hosting a gaming club where all students can come to participate and casually play together in an environment where toxicity is not tolerated, you can help these students gain confidence and connect with other gamers in the school. From this, these students may then decide to try out for your esports team.

Team Bonding Strategies

Your new esports team may know each other and play well together, but more than likely, students will need to build relationships with their teammates. They are gamers, so you will need to embrace that identity with an icebreaker.

Did you know that gamers take on different roles in games? Games such as *Paladins* label those roles. In *Paladins*, players are Front Line, Damage, Support, and Flank. In games like *Overwatch*, players take on roles such as Tank, Healer, and Damage. The Tank is a defensive role: the player can absorb large amounts of damage so their teammates can execute more complicated attacks. The Healer is a support role, acting to keep the team alive while relying on the other players to destroy their foes. The Damage player can deal heavy damage to opponents but relies on the Tank and Healer to survive.

Have your students create a list of all the team-based games they have played and generate a list of "roles" for each game that are similar to the roles of Tank, Healer, and Damage from *Overwatch*. This activity builds insight for both coaches and players. As the coach, you will know how to balance your players into teams for scrimmages. Your players will find peers who complement their gameplay styles. A player who wants to be in the forward position in *Rocket League* wants to be paired with someone who likes to play back in goal. Although all players in *Rocket League* typically need to be adaptable for all zones of play, balancing your players based on interest and personality will create sets of complementary players.

Games can build trust among people. To play a game, you trust that your opponent will play a sportsmanlike game and graciously win or lose. That trust is not exclusive to video games; you can build it with any type of game. However, video games tend to identify a winner and a loser, and your team may frequently practice among themselves, frequently creating winners and losers. You may not think students who lost a scrimmage will be affected by it, but you'll notice that players tend to win/lose in streaks. Coming back from a loss in esports can be difficult because of the negative feelings after a loss. You need an icebreaker that is a game but doesn't divide your players into winners and losers.

Select a cooperative board game, such as Forbidden Island or Pandemic, in which all the players either win together or lose together. These games also require frequent communication among players, who must coordinate all their actions across multiple turns. Set aside an hour for your players to bond via a co-op board game, and their sense of unity will grow.

Expanding the Pipeline

An esports team is a great chance to empower students' CTE. Since esports is the fastest growing industry in the world, it is important that students know that they can turn their love of video games into careers, especially STEM careers. As educators, we need to create what's known as a pipeline that esports athletes can follow to get from middle school through college and into a career by following their passion for gaming.

Chris has a team behind the esports team to help build out the esports ecosystem. Chris's team consists of both players and other support staff that fill vital support roles on the esports team, such as shoutcaster, IT specialist, scout, statistician, graphic designer, video editor, event planner, journalist, accountant, marketer, and many more. By giving students the jobs that need to be done to run a successful esports team, you provide hands-on experience with possible careers they might someday want to explore.

JUST LIKE DRIVING A RACE CAR

While it's easy to draw an analogy between sports in terms of the roles that team members play, it can be a little trickier with esports. After all, there are an incredible number of roles that a student on an esports team can play. Kevin Brown, esports program specialist from the Orange County Department of Education and NASEF, compares esports to NASCAR. Now, while that may seem a bit curious at first, Kevin explains it this way:

> If we think of just a car and a driver and five hundred left-hand turns—that's not NASCAR, there's so much more that goes on. You've got a pit crew, you've got a fuel scientist, you've got a coach in your ear telling you how to take the lap, you've got some guy reading the tire pressure and heat till you want to swap out. There's an ambulance sitting off to the side in case somebody eats the concrete. Everybody up in the stands selling concessions.

> There's a world of work that goes into NASCAR, and so it is with esports. Once that's established, you realize that there are established pathways to get into those kinds of work. Whether or not you live in esports and go on to become some part of the magical machine, there are careers that exist anywhere in industry. So if you learn event planning, sure, you could fire off and make a great esports event at a high school, at a college, or a pro event, no doubt, but that same skill set can be parlayed into catering and banquet management, and hotels and restaurants and tourism. So there is a way to become an event planner on any scale. Whether or not you work in esports, the skills you learn can be applied anywhere else.

Besides the competition element, the students on Chris's team play local colleges so that afterward the college players can talk about what they are majoring in and how their passion for gaming plays a part in their choice. Chris's students leave feeling inspired after talking to the college students about their shared passion. The students who may not think college is an option for them start realizing that maybe they want to go to college because they can continue to pursue esports at the collegiate level and then graduate into a career, traditional or otherwise, that lets them continue in gaming. The esports pipeline we build can carry our kids through to college and beyond.

Building the school-to-college pipeline is also a good way to reach those students without an existing home-school connection. Students who are interested in esports often aren't involved in other after-school sports, activities, and clubs. When Chris started his esports team at Knollwood Middle School in September 2018, nearly his entire team had no home-school connection. They weren't involved in extracurricular activities. Once the school day was over, his kids went home. The research is clear that involvement in school extracurriculars leads to better student development and learning. An esports team presents an opportunity to reach more students and let them know they are valued and their passions are important. Esports is another way to let kids know they matter. Like many traditional sports, many esports teams find value in connecting grades, attendance, and behavior with being eligible to take part in esports. In other words, being part of an esports team can motivate students to stay on the straight and narrow, just like the motivation behind playing traditional sports.

Steve has heard from many parents who say that their child loves being part of the gaming community at school despite not having many friends outside of school. Parents also ask about students their children are interacting with in the game club so that they can look to better support their child in creating friendships that extend outside of school. The game club/esports program provides a social network for children who may not otherwise be proficient at navigating the social world of school.

The EsportsEDU Community

If we've learned anything as connected educators, it's that people are our greatest resource and constructivist learning is where it's at! When people talk about their PLN (professional learning network), they often refer to the idea that we are better together. If you are just starting an esports program you may want to consider finding other coaches to network with on Twitter using the #esportsedu hashtag, or by joining our Esports in Education Discord at https://bit.ly/esportsedudiscord. Having a network of coaches to bounce ideas off of or give you advice is always valuable, especially when first starting a team. The #esportsedu hashtag and Discord are also great places to find scrimmages and matches.

As we write this, the Discord community has close to a thousand members representing all esports in education stakeholder groups, including students, parents, educators, coaches, counselors, administrators, and league organizers, and all levels, including elementary education, secondary ed, higher ed, and even professional esports. You can also participate in the #esportsedu interactive chat hosted by Jim O'Hagen, Carrie Linden, and friends on Thursday nights from 7:30 to 8:30 p.m. ET on http://www.twitch.tv/taoesports. The chat is comprised of a live discussion among the hosts with the opportunity for viewers to engage.

The online community is incredibly generous and happy to help, whether you are trying to start an esports program or find a league or scrimmage for your team. People in the community have been through it all and made many of the common mistakes so you don't have to! The wealth of knowledge and support is incredible.

BECOME A CONDUCTOR

Starting an esports program can seem like a daunting task for anyone, particularly if you do not come from a gaming background. However, Dr. Chris Haskell suggests that putting yourself in the right mindset can help anyone become an esports coach. As Doc puts it:

> Like the scientist in every disaster movie, I discovered there was this massive asteroid hurtling toward us, about to explode. And that asteroid was esports. At that time seventeen different universities had varsity programs, and there were a whole bunch poised to come in. So I took that argument to the university president. "Mr. President, there's a huge asteroid coming toward the campus and we ought to mobilize, or it could be a disaster, and we'll get left behind." And the president said, "Okay." And a moment later, I realized I'm on a rocket with Bruce Willis.

> What do you do? I was, in my former life, before coming to the university, a high school band director. And I have come to understand that esports is very much like a band—thankfully, without the oboes. As a director of esports, you are preparing students for a performance that you can only somewhat control. You can increase or decrease the tempo, and you can play with the dynamics. But beyond that, it's in their hands. And how well you prepare them to play their role, to play their part, is critical to their success. And to me, that's really cool.

Mentors can also be found at the collegiate level. Almost every college has some sort of esports team or club. Many institutions have been receptive to mentoring middle or secondary school esports programs. For example, the FH Knights have a tradition of playing a "mix-it-up" match, where teams of schoolchildren play against students from the

Rutgers University esports team. Afterward, the Rutgers students talk about their college experience, future plans, and how esports fits into that equation. Consider reaching out to colleges or universities for guidance. Building a relationship with higher institutions has the added benefit of helping grow the school-to-college esports pipeline, a goal of the #esportsedu movement.

Beyond college esports are professional esports teams like the New York Excelsior. Some educators have had success reaching out to pro teams, pro leagues, and even the game developers themselves for support and learning opportunities for their students.

RUNNING AN ESPORTS PRACTICE

Generally, the average practice session at the collegiate level seems to be between 90 and 120 minutes, two to three days per week, and students play together in their free time, too. Esports practices can be broken down into four main parts: drills, situational awareness, live competition, and video review and reflection.

Drills

Drilling is the frequent repetition of important skills in an effort to improve the quality and effectiveness of those skills. Think of it as focusing on the basic actions in an attempt to get better, faster, and stronger at that action. In football, drills might include footwork or ball-handling drills for running backs, filling and tackling drills for linebackers, tip drills for defensive backs, or double-team drills for defensive linemen. These make up the fundamental skills players need to be successful in their position. In esports, drilling is no less vital. Low-skill players can improve through drilling.

In *Rocket League*, for example, players can go to the training area of the game and take part in both developer-created and community-created drills that focus on three fundamentals skills necessary to be good at

Rocket League: goalkeeping, aerials, and shooting. Each video game has its own basic skills that students should try to master. Players' performance in games that require aiming, dodging, or combining keystrokes in a fast, efficient manner (usually called actions per minute, or APM) can all be improved by drilling.

If your game has a training mode, like *Rocket League*, tracking player performance over time is valuable. If your game doesn't have built-in training areas, it is up to you as the coach to come up with drills and a way to determine student growth from drills. Drilling is a great way to warm up at the start of esports practice, just as it is in other sports. Drilling at the start of practice is also a great way to spend time while waiting for players to show up or get set up for practice. Drilling as an anchor activity before starting the team-based portion of practice is an effective use of time.

Situational Awareness

Having situational awareness is a combination of two factors. First, situational awareness is the ability to know something is happening and, second, reacting appropriately to the situation. In baseball, situational awareness means running on contact if there are two outs. It means telling the second baseman to be ready to turn a double play when there is one out and a runner on first. In wrestling, it might be acting appropriately if your opponent has gotten behind you and is trying to return you to the mat. In soccer, it means knowing what to do on a corner kick. Every sport has commonly occurring situations that need to be recognized and reacted to correctly. Consistently reacting quickly and appropriately to common game situations is often the key to victory. Esports is no different, but also unique when it comes to situational awareness.

In esports, there is a phenomenon called the meta. The meta is the current strongest strategy being used to win in a video game. In *Overwatch*, there was a time when 2-2-2 was the meta. This meant that an *Overwatch* team made up of two healers, two tanks, and two DPS (characters who deal high damage per second) characters were what most teams used to try and win. Over time, usually pushed forward by professional esports players at the highest skill level or updates (patches) that change the rules of the game, the meta evolves. After the 2-2-2 meta came the dive meta. The dive meta was when a team used a composition of fast-moving, mobile characters to attack their opponents when on offense. Currently the *Overwatch* meta is running three tanks and three support characters. This incarnation of the *Overwatch* meta is called GOATS. In each shift in the meta, players have to adapt to and prepare for the new meta.

Developing situational awareness, again, involves two parts: identifying and reacting. To identify the current GOATS meta, players must be trained to know what characters make up the GOATS meta, because being able to identify GOATS is the first step to defending the strategy. After players know how to identify a situation, they must learn to react appropriately. Defending GOATS may include strategies that create space between themselves and the GOATS team, since a GOATS team generally wants to be in your face. It can also mean changing team composition to use more mobile, damaging characters to defend against GOATS.

Regardless of the game or the current meta, the point is that almost every esports game has a strong strategy that is popular with most players. The best way to find the current meta for your game is to watch pro matches and listen to casters calling the game, as the meta is often a topic of discussion. You can also check official forums, Reddit, and YouTube to find players discussing the current meta.[6]

While professional players are sometimes the catalyst for a change in the meta, it is more likely that the meta will evolve through changes/patches to the game made by the developers. Video game developers often discuss upcoming changes to a game before the changes go live. As a coach, you and your players should be following upcoming patches to your game. Tracking patch changes will allow you to predict how nerfs (the weakening of champions) and buffs (the strengthening of champions) may change the meta and ultimately how you identify and react to common situations in a game.

Scrimmages and Video Review and Reflection

Live competitions, often called scrimmages, are practice games played against members of the same team or against other teams. Scrimmages are usually done under the same conditions real matches would be played, and they are often recorded. Afterward, these recordings are used to break down and analyze player performance.

The goal of video review and reflection in esports is to help players identify both errors and excellence in decision-making on an individual player level and on a team level. Usually scrimmages and matches are recorded and broken down by the coach. The coach may focus on a particular situation and help players work through strengths and weaknesses in gameplay as an entire team, or an individual level. Reflecting on gameplay can be done verbally or through writing prompts, which are likely unique to esports in education.

TIPS FROM THE FIELD

FOCUS IS THE KEY

Brock Cheung is a student at the University of Missouri who also coaches high school esports. And while he practices his gaming skills and works on improving his ranking, he spends just as much time honing his coaching strategies, as well. What he has learned is that, just as in traditional sports, where emphasis and practice need to be placed on individual skills, so it is with esports:

> A little bit of my methodology when I coach is that I take a VOD (video on demand) of a player. It's basically a film of their game play. And I watch it; I point out the things that they're doing wrong, just like any other coach would do. However, first I try to bring up the issues as questions. I ask the players why they thought they did something or why did they do something. Because I want them to see their logic, and then the error of

their logic if there was something wrong. So that way they can process it in their head as a way of, like, "Okay, this is the correct logic, and this is why this was this."

After we review the VOD, I summarize three or four things they need to work on, so they're not working on all fifty things at once. They're working on three to four consistent things. This focuses them, so they're, like, "Okay, I'm gonna work on this thing right now." And they go in and they work on that thing right now, and they'll keep working on it until it's improved. After that's done, they'll give me a new VOD. Then I'm like, "Okay, here's three or four more things you can work on."

So it's a step-by-step approach, more than anything, and that's how people—at least the people I've coached—have learned.

FINDING MATCHES AND JOINING A LEAGUE

Esports is still new at the high school level and brand new at the elementary and middle school level, which means that a coach will often have to find their own matches. The two best places to find another team to play is using the #esportsedu on Twitter and joining our Discord server. Sometimes finding competition can be hard, so don't forget to keep in mind a key area esports differs from traditional sports: there is no travel cost. Don't be afraid to plan matches with teams from different parts of the country or even different parts of the world. While it may take creative scheduling to make the time work, there is nothing stopping you from taking your esports team global.

A variety of organizations are vying for governorship and/or market share of esports in education. Some are for-profit; some are nonprofit. It is up to you to decide if joining a league is right for your team. Below are the most popular leagues in esports for education:

- North American Scholastic Esports Federation (NASEF)—
  NASEF is the only esports for education league that is free to
  schools.[7] This nonprofit was born out of the Orange County
  High School esports scene and is staffed mostly by current or
  former educators. NASEF "was rooted in providing Orange
  County high school students with the opportunity to pursue
  their interests, develop a greater community, and enhance their
  skills in leadership, teamwork, problem-solving and communication. Now, in our second year, we are moving forward as
  the North America Scholastic Esports Federation to go above
  and beyond."
- National Federation of State High School Association (NFHS)—
  From their website: "The National Federation of State High
  School Associations (NFHS) and the NFHS Network have
  entered into a partnership with PlayVS to begin the rollout of
  esports competition in high schools throughout the nation.
  PlayVS, an online gaming provider, will work directly with the
  NFHS and the NFHS Network to introduce esports to high
  schools and state associations beginning this fall, with an initial
  rollout in at least fifteen states. After regular-season competition
  between schools on the PlayVS online platform, state championship games will be played before a live spectator audience and
  streamed on the NFHS Network." [8]
- High School Esports League (HSEL)—From their website: "The
  High School Esports Partnership Program is a partnership
  between the HSEL and your school to bring it exclusive perks.
  This includes but is not limited to Premium Tournaments,
  Sponsored LAN Parties, Twitch.tv broadcasting incentives and
  much more."[9]
- National Association of College Esports (NACE)—Though only
  involved at the collegiate level, NACE deserves a mention because
  they are the closest thing to a true governing body that esports
  in education has right now. NACE is slowly gaining recognition

as the governing body for esports at the collegiate level. While the NCAA has been talking about getting into esports,[10] NACE has been gaining market share. Whether or not NACE becomes the governing body of middle school and high school programs remains to be seen, but it is an organization to keep an eye on and take cues from.

- Tespa—Formerly the Texas Esports Association, this is a North American collegiate esports organization headquartered in the offices of Blizzard Entertainment in Irvine, California. Founded in 2012 as a collegiate gaming club at the University of Texas at Austin, Tespa expanded nationally in 2013 as an event-support network for college gaming organizations. In 2014, the company announced an official partnership with Blizzard Entertainment, hosting online leagues for *Hearthstone, League of Legends, StarCraft II, Heroes of the Storm,* and *Overwatch.*[11]

- The Electronic Gaming Federation (EGF)—From their website: "EGF provides the definitive infrastructure for interscholastic esports. With students at the center, EGF's collegiate and high school leagues and programs are designed with inspiration from the best aspects of traditional sports to provide the platform for students to make their mark in esports."[12]

These organizations are all vying for a foothold in esports in the education space. The space is still wide open and consists of a number of private for-profit organizations, as well as a number of grassroots organizations that are emerging to support the students that they serve. Some organizations are well-funded, and others are taking more of a bootstrap approach. We are definitely experiencing an interesting rise of esports, and many want to be part of the growth.

WHAT ABOUT MIDDLE SCHOOLS?

As we look at the development of esports programs, we see many similarities to traditional sports programs. College programs certainly paved the way, creating an obvious need to develop a feeder program for prospective college recruits. It became clear that we needed high school esports programs to develop competitive gamers and prepare them for opportunities in college. The boom in high school programs answered this call. There's no question that high school esports is alive and well and not going anywhere! Of course this begs the next question: How do we get students interested and prepared for high school programs?

We are currently seeing a surge in middle school programs through the growth of casual game clubs and competitive esports programs (and some trying to serve both purposes). The goal is providing safe spaces for like-minded kids to explore esports and gain experience in competitive gaming. We have a ways to go at the middle school level in terms of organization and league management. While many middle schools have traditional sports programs as feeders to high school programs, they often are not as organized as they are on the high school level.

At this time, esports at the middle school level is like the Wild West: anything goes. There are no governing bodies or organizations accepting middle schools into their program, and there doesn't seem to be anything coming anytime soon. Middle school programs will need to find their own matches and create their own leagues. The recommended path for middle schools is to follow collegiate and high school best practices. As coach of the FH Knights middle school team, Chris has created a site with his students called Esports For Edu, which aims to be a free league focused on middle school (and high school) teams around the world as a place to find each other, plan matches, and keep records.[13] In addition, the New Jersey NASEF affiliate, Garden State Esports, founded by Chris and Steve, has every intention of growing esports at the elementary and middle school level.

Middle school esports is growing at a rapid pace, primarily through the grassroots movement started by Chris. Matches are happening among teams across the country, and the community demonstrates a great passion for providing opportunities for middle school students. Programs at the primary (elementary) level are not far behind as we continue to focus on developing a scalable K–12–through–college pipeline. Soon enough, there will be sanctioned organizations supporting esports at all levels.

THINKING OUTSIDE THE SCHOOL BOX

Just as education happens in a variety of environments, so can scholastic esports. While many teams are formed in schools, community-based organizations have the opportunity to participate as well.

After-School Clubs

In a 2018 press release from NASEF, Jeff Davis, executive director of the California AfterSchool Network, talks about the learning benefits of esports in after-school settings:

> Today's students will have the opportunity to solve critical issues and participate in a workforce that is nearly unrecognizable to us today. After-school providers understand the importance of offering hands-on STEM learning opportunities to prepare students for the evolving future. Esports offers a way to engage students through gaming, while teaching them skills that will be important to their future success.
>
> Today's students enjoy gaming, but few may understand the career opportunities gaming represents, from professional game play to coding and engineering the next wave of innovative video games. Beyond those industry-specific careers, a wealth of opportunities will be available to students who have developed esports skills, like data analysis, digital imaging, web development, journalism, event management, and more.[14]

Local Libraries

Libraries are a wonderful example of institutions adapting to meet the needs of their users. Most libraries have added areas where users can access the internet, and many have started lending more than books. Around the country, libraries have started lending tools, toys, and even video games. A few libraries have started using video games, in the form of tournaments and esports teams, to draw more people to the library, a trend seen in schools as well. It should come as no surprise, then, that libraries are a great home for esports teams.

The Cherokee Public Library in Cherokee, Iowa, integrated esports into their work on a project focused on supporting middle school students on college and career awareness. As the Cherokee library researched the needs of middle schoolers they learned that local businesses found teen workers were lacking in soft skills, such as the ability to communicate clearly with team members, stay on task, and adapt to older technology. Surveying the middle school population for their interests led to the discovery that all had an interest in playing video games or played video games regularly. Some had even played video games the day of the survey, which was at ten in the morning. Thus recognizing a need, the Cherokee library's esports team was born.

When the program got up and running, they had team members work on a number of projects, including creating résumés featuring their favorite game characters and identifying skills the characters possessed in various video games. This particular activity tied in well with esports, as it allowed team members to discuss their passions in games and share their favorite game characters while honing life skills. Along with activities like résumé writing, the Cherokee Public Library collaborated with community partners to facilitate esports program activities. (At the same time, community members were able to build relationships with the teens and help them learn about different job opportunities in the area.). The curriculum leveraged to drive the program was offered through NASEF and helped the library connect esports with community activities and related careers, such as graphic and web design, journalism, coding, streaming, entrepreneurship, and shoutcasting.

Developing outcomes and assessments for library-hosted esports can be challenging, particularly if the information collected is more qualitative than quantitative. To that end, Cherokee library staff struc-tured assessment tools that reflected the interest of esports participants. Talk-back boards served as a clever way to gain insight on a topic, and the library staff have used them in the past to gauge interest and outcomes of programming. They particularly utilized talk-back boards when team members were working on identifying when they were frustrated with a particular aspect of a game or another player. Library staff also experi-mented with utilizing memes as a medium for a talk-back board where team members would caption a meme with how it related to a particu-lar concept. Meme templates can easily be found online, and relevant memes can be found on popular forums like Reddit

Team members compiled gaming tips, original art, comics, and memes about concepts they had learned in the esports team pertaining to soft skills and technology in the form of a small zine (a homemade, typically web-based magazine). The zine also functions to recruit team members who may not be avid gamers, but who like to edit and cre-ate. They too can learn future-ready skills by collaborating, utilizing and learning new technology, and serving as a contact to distribute and print the zine.

Cherokee Public Library's trial run of an esports team went so well that the team members and their siblings began to lobby their schools for programming. In collaboration with the library, the school district launched an after-school esports program with a grounding in STEM curricula. Players primarily focused on Nintendo gaming systems, incor-porating strong math principles to break down statistics of matches, players, characters, and maps for *Super Smash Bros. Ultimate.* Players also had a chance to test their computational thinking with projects in Scratch, as well as learn web and design basics to supplement their own online activities. Given student enthusiasm for the project, school administrators are discussing having esports and STEM as an activity in school on a rotation, like art, music, and physical education.

CUT SCENE ——————————————————

THE IMPACT OF A PANDEMIC
ON LIBRARY PROGRAMS

As the COVID-19 pandemic shut down many libraries within the US, the Cherokee Public Library in Iowa was no exception. After the governor halted the school year for students in mid-March, libraries in Iowa also started to transition from serving patrons inside the library to a curbside and digital model of providing access to materials and enrichment. For the Cherokee Public Library's esports coach and librarian, Tyler Hahn, this was an opportunity to reimagine how esports could engage a community.

Because he could not physically meet with his esports team, called KEE+Control, in the library, Tyler (another NASEF Fellow) pivoted to engaging his esports team not only through online matches from home, but also through bonus objectives—weekly esports challenges for his team, and anyone else in the community, to take on. Each week, Tyler posts a different bonus objective on social media, the team Discord chat, and on public-access television to reach a wide swath of the community.

Participants can send or tag the library with their completed project. Each week, the winning project is announced by the library and given a small prize. Each project can be completed with either a tech or no/low tech option, in order to be fair to anyone without access to data or the internet at home. Some weekly challenges are as simple as drawing or creating characters inspired by favorite video games, while others are to create 3-D models or objects out of household materials. From a STEM perspective, esports team members are also challenged to figure out data on win/loss percentages, average match times per map, and the calculated probability of team members' victory chances against one another. Tyler's esports athletes also contribute by voting on which bonus submissions they like the best. By engaging members of the community through esports, Tyler hopes that when the library is open again, patrons will be excited to learn more about esports.

The library has also undertaken a major project in organizing a drive-in gaming tournament for which consoles will be connected to projectors. From there, families would pull their cars into parking spaces near the screen and compete against one another, while people in cars in the queue to play can officiate and cheer on the players.

Community-Based Organizations

Other local organizations, like the Boys & Girls Clubs of America and YMCA, are also implementing scholastic esports clubs. In fact, the YMCA of Orange County, California, started more than forty NASEF clubs. They use NASEF materials to provide gaming clubs in a safe, educational, and fun environment facilitated through organized, multiplayer video game competitions.

The YMCA Scholastic Esports program serves today's youth by providing opportunities for all students to use esports as a platform to acquire critical communication, collaboration, and problem-solving skills to thrive in work and in life. Rather than solely focusing on competition, the program is introducing students to the wide variety of roles so they can expand their skills and gain real experience in future potential career aspirations.

LOOKING TO
THE FUTURE

Esports is a growing industry that shows little to no sign of slowing or regressing. As the industry keeps growing, it is filling niches that are left void by traditional sports. Looking at the future of esports, it's hard not to reflect on what the impact of the coronavirus pandemic will be.

COVID-19 AND ESPORTS

The COVID-19 pandemic is a prime example of a space where esports filled a need at a time when traditional sports were entirely grounded. As sporting events globally were brought to a screeching halt during the pandemic due to social distancing and quarantine mandates, esports continued providing an outlet for folks, both competitors and viewers. This was strengthened by many of the world's best-known athletes taking to the gaming platforms themselves for competition and play.

Many industries used esports to maintain and connect with their audience while everyone was stuck at home. With the traditional sports world shut down, networks like ESPN packed their schedule with more and more esports content. Even the sports leagues themselves turned to esports for content. NASCAR's new esports league, eNASCAR, held their first event: the *iRacing* Pro Invitational Series. It was a massive success, drawing the largest TV audience for an esports event yet. The NBA hosted an *NBA 2K* Players Tournament, in which NBA stars competed in head-to-head matchups with the money raised going to COVID-19 relief charities. FIFA worked on developing a 128-team esports tournament, and the NHL will be simulating the rest of their season for fans in their video game, *NHL 20*. Twitch, the streaming platform where many students watch their favorite gamers, broke records during the time of stay-at-home orders. And while recruiting was all but halted for the military, the navy began using its esports team, Goats & Glory, to attract potential recruits.

The same thing happened internationally. Motor racing quickly replaced their scheduled driver-and-vehicle events with the virtual Grand Prix, hosted by Formula 1. In fact, Ferrari driver Charles Leclerc won his debut race for the FDA Hublot Esports Team, drawing both interest and continued allegiance from many Formula 2 fans. The race was broadcast live on ESPN2 during twelve hours of esports programming. Similarly, many National Rugby League (NRL) clubs, including the Canterbury-Bankstown Bulldogs and Wests Tigers, took to the *Fortnite* environment to compete in a livestream on Facebook, during what would have been a key time during their traditional season. The Finnish Elite League took a similar approach, migrating their league playoffs from the ice to the *NHL 20* console game. Esports has allowed fans to continue to feel connected to the sport and the athletes, and has continued to foster brand loyalty, while the traditional modes of competition are completely halted.

These new revenue streams for these typically nongaming sports have helped ease the financial burden of the social distancing/quarantine circumstances. "Most of our traditional streams of revenue are almost tapped out," said Nigel Smart, the Adelaide Football Club's chief operating officer, on the *Sports Geek* podcast last year. "Where does future growth come from? We have a multidimensional international strategy, and we also have a multicultural strategy. Having an esports team is an extension of both of those. The founding shareholders of Legacy [Esport], they're still involved in the team. They're on the performance side, they're on the front end. What we bring as a football club is that back end in terms of content strategy, merchandise models, and commercial partnerships."

While the current relationship between the esports world and traditional sports may feel like a bit of an arranged marriage, forced out of necessity, there is a fair chance that the future will prove fruitful as a result.[1]

COVID-19 AND EDUCATION

Of course the virus didn't just create problems for sports. It created unprecedented challenges for schools around the globe. Many schools closed for part of the school year, which made finding ways to connect with students more important than ever. Teachers looked to platforms such as Google Meet, Flipgrid, and Zoom to maintain face-to-face relationships with students, and some schools found an additional way to keep up with their students: esports!

Because they're online, most school esports programs were able to continue even in the face of a global pandemic, when schools switched to remote learning. The fact that esports were used to engage and connect with students while schools were closed shouldn't be surprising. Esports has become the athletics of remote living.

Taking a page from these examples, educators, coaches, and players used the pandemic as a chance to show how esports can be a platform to keep us together even when all other opportunities seem shut down.

The Show Goes On

The COVID-19 situation presented challenges as well as opportunities for Steve's team. From the start of the quarantine, Steve had no intention of stopping his esports activities. In a time when everyone was trying to maintain some sense of normalcy and educators were looking to provide meaningful activities for our students, Steve saw esports as a necessity.

The transition to a home-based esports team was tough at first. Steve had a difficult time organizing his team from home and establishing a practice and match schedule. To better communicate with his team, he decided to set up a Discord server so they could continue to connect. Through Discord, a group-chatting platform originally built for gamers, communities can be easily built to allow for voice, text, and video chatting. He also created a Google classroom. He used Google Classroom for his classes, so it made sense to use the tool for the students on his team. Best of all, it leveraged a platform that his students were already familiar with.

Another nice aspect of Google Classroom for Steve was the ability to embed a Google Meet for athletes within Google Classroom. Steve moved his game-club meetings online via Google Meet, which allowed the group to come together twice a week to see one another face-to-face and do some real-time gaming together. Bringing his students together through Google Classroom and Discord worked better than Steve anticipated. Students made matches and played games together even outside the times Steve had designated. One of his seventh-grade students, Tristan, said that when he and his teammates are not doing schoolwork, "the team is always trying to play awesome games together and get to know each other better."

One of the tournaments Steve's team entered from home was a competitive *Minecraft* tournament. The primary game in competitive *Minecraft* is Capture the Wool, which plays like a typical capture the flag game. Teams of five work together to attack their opponents' base and return to their base with the flag while also defending their own base. Players find materials and weapons to use in the match. It's a fast-paced and exciting game that definitely brings *Minecraft* right into the esports arena. With a little guidance from Steve, his students formed a team, registered, and competed on a regular basis in *Minecraft* tournaments. Another marquee matchup for Steve's esports team was a *Rocket League* doubleheader against James Monroe Middle School and Eisenhower Middle School, both in Albuquerque, New Mexico. The event was organized by the students from home.

Esports for Everyone

As students were looking for opportunities to continue participating in esports activities, organizations like the Texas Scholastic Esports Federation (TexSEF) answered the call with a series of weekly tournaments for middle and high school students that could be played from home.[2]

Instructional coach and NASEF fellow J. D. Williams, from Laveen Elementary School in Phoenix, Arizona, used esports to connect with not just his esports team, but his entire community. In the fall of 2019, J. D. started an esports club at Laveen with fifth- to eighth-grade students playing *Rocket League* after school, twice a week. When J. D.'s school closed in March 2020 for the rest of the school year because of COVID-19, he wanted to continue engaging his esports athletes and draw in his entire community through online games. To that end, he started hosting and streaming community game nights in April, continuing them throughout Arizona's Stay Home, Stay Healthy, Stay Connected executive order.

J. D. started small, with a few trial runs of *Rocket League* tournaments with his esports team and school staff members. *Rocket League* has built-in tournaments, which allows J. D. to spectate and shoutcast his team's games. After the test tournaments were successful, J. D. advertised a game night through his school's Facebook page and Google classrooms and invited students and staff from another middle school with an esports to club to play in the competition. The number of players who participated in the weekly tournaments grew each week.

Even though the *Rocket League* tournaments were engaging some of his students, J. D. felt he was still not giving as many students the opportunity to participate as he could, because *Rocket League* needs to be purchased. J. D. wanted to find a free-to-play title that any student with a video game system and internet access could play. After talking with his esports team, coaches, and his school principal, he settled on a title you may have heard of: *Fortnite*.

Many schools are hesitant to engage students through *Fortnite*. J. D. did have some concerns because *Fortnite* is a third-person shooter with an ESRB rating of T. He made sure that he communicated with parents about the teen rating and how to decide if a game is appropriate for their child.

Another issue with *Fortnite* was getting all of the students into the same game at the same time. Luckily J. D. was accepted into Epic's Support-A-Creator program, which permits custom *Fortnite* matches that students can join with a match code. In his first *Fortnite* event, J. D. had over forty students join the match from home. Friday Night *Fortnite* has been a huge hit for J. D.'s community, and it gets bigger every week.

J. D.'s weekly community game nights have allowed him and fellow teachers who have joined him to continue to give their students and community a connection to their school that wouldn't be possible without online gaming and esports. J. D.'s seventh-grade student Nicholas said, "Esports is different from all of the other school sport activities. I've gotten better at the games and am able to socialize without going out somewhere. I like the amount of social interaction, and it is easier to make friends than I thought."

Engaging Students with Meaningful Activities

During the COVID-19 pandemic, educators and esports organizations got creative and found ways to continue to engage students from home. This involved the continuation of competition where possible, the development of short-term tournaments, and initiatives to move from competition to community in this important time of transition. NASEF partnered with their Florida and New Jersey affiliates by offering a number of *Minecraft* Build Challenges related to COVID-19. This project was spearheaded by Erik Leitner from Broward County Schools, along with Steve and Cathy Cheo-Isaacs. The program was introduced through a number of livestream sessions produced by Mike Washburn and the web platform Participate. The idea was to leverage student interest while providing opportunities to create and publish work as individuals and teams. The *Minecraft* COVID Build Challenges were posted to http://flipgrid.com/minecraftcovid19, allowing students to record and post their contest submissions.

The challenges included:

- *Minecraft* **Stuck at Home Challenge:** Build your dream home for the duration of the social distancing.
- **What is COVID-19?:** Build a model of the virus.
- **Future Medical Facility:** Design and build a medical facility that can handle the challenges we are facing.
- **Inform the Public:** Design a library or museum to share information about the virus and dispel misinformation.

- **Escape/Entry Room:** Design an escape room full of challenges that allows the player to enter the restroom to wash their hands.
- **COVID-19 Rube Goldberg Machine:** Create a Rube Goldberg machine that provides a complex device to solve a simple problem related to COVID-19.

All this also prompted the generation of some best practices on facilitating student engagement during remote learning:

1. **Provide choice:** Allow students to choose the activities they want to engage in.
2. **Keep it simple:** People often find it difficult to navigate all the new technology thrown at them. Use platforms that students are familiar with. Many are playing *Minecraft*, and Flipgrid provides an easy way for students to submit their work. However, not everyone is familiar with Flipgrid, so permit alternate means of submission so everyone can participate without being frustrated by the technology.
3. **Build community around the projects:** Projects were shared via social media, the NASEF community, and other vehicles, to spread the word. Interested teachers also shared the challenges with their students. The Flipgrid portal allows people to see other approved submissions, making it easy to share with a wider audience.
4. **Make activities meaningful and relevant:** The COVID-19 pandemic affected everyone. These activities allowed students to use tools they love, like *Minecraft*, while touching on SEL and other skills to provide meaning and an outlet.
5. **Celebrate the accomplishments:** All students who entered one of the challenges and met the criteria got their class entered in a drawing for a prize package of ten HyperX gaming headsets. One prize package was awarded for each challenge. Also, as submissions were accepted, the videos were shared through a variety of social media platforms to celebrate the students' work.[3]

These challenges created an opportunity for students to be creative and engage in light competition. Soon after they were released, the challenges were translated into Spanish, shared with the NASEF partners in Mexico City, and made available to all Spanish-speaking students to allow for broader participation.

Engaging Everyone with Meaningful Activities

Professional sports organizations took a leaf from education and decided to engage fans in similar ways while they were on hiatus. NASEF and its affiliates worked together to create the *Minecraft* Face-Off, a series of build challenges related to hockey.[4] This time, the group collaborated with professional hockey organizations. The first partner on board was the Anaheim Ducks, which took a lead in developing the program with NASEF. The idea was shared with other organizations, and quickly the Vegas Golden Knights and the Detroit Red Wings got on board. Participants were tasked with three challenges:

1. **Hockey Team Logo Design Challenge:** Recreate (or reimagine) your favorite hockey team logo in *Minecraft*! Will you build it block by block, code it, or snazz it up in your own way?

2. **Hockey Jersey Design Challenge:** Redesign your favorite hockey team's jersey in *Minecraft*! What elements would you include in your custom jersey? Will you incorporate a new logo, color scheme, or mascot?

3. **Hockey Arena Design Challenge:** It's the year 2120, and your favorite hockey team is accepting proposals for their new arena. Design and build your ultimate hockey arena in *Minecraft*! Will your venue be used exclusively for hockey, or will it have multiple uses? Where will it be? How will fans be transported to it? How will they purchase concessions and merch?

Once again, the challenges were livestreamed with the help of Participate. Competitors had two weeks to complete and submit their builds via

Flipgrid. This is a model that can engage fans in any professional sport and will likely lead to additional opportunities for the gaming community.

Another *Minecraft*-related competitive option launched by NASEF during COVID-19 was *Minecraft* Masters, an international event in which teams entered a build based on a theme. Four teams were selected to move on to the Masters Competition, a round robin tournament involving three unique build challenges leading to the final, which featured the first and second place countries going head-to-head. The round robin and finals matches were based on events like the LEGO Masters and FIRST Robotics competitions. This competition focused on creativity, design, engineering, and coding. The *Minecraft* Masters also offered @Home challenges so that anyone interested could participate and submit their builds alongside the teams competing live. A junior division allowed students under the age of thirteen to compete.

Minecraft *Meets Competitive Gaming*

CompMC is a group of college students with a passion for *Minecraft* and esports. They developed a number of competitive *Minecraft* maps that bring all the excitement of any competitive game to *Minecraft*. Their featured game mode is *Capture the Wool*, in which there are a variety of maps. Each team attempts to steal the wool from the other base and return it to their base while defending their base and, most importantly, their wool. The typical match is 5–5 and really demonstrates the importance of team play. In order to help keep school groups engaged during COVID-19, they hosted pickup games on their server every Saturday and a large tournament called April Ambush, which brought more than thirty teams together for a full weekend of competitive *Minecraft*.

Whether by keeping the esports season going while students and teachers are home or keeping fandom alive during the pandemic, esports is clearly the athletics of remote learning. The coronavirus will have lasting effects on our lives. Hopefully, one of those lasting effects will be the understanding that whether we're in school or learning from a distance, every community can benefit from engaging in esports.

WHAT COMES NEXT?

Let's end by taking a moment to imagine how esports will shift, taking it from being identified as "esports" to being identified as "a sport." First, like traditional athletes, esports athletes are seen as athletes by the US government, applying as just an "athlete" for government-issued visas. Second, the world begs the question: Will esports make its way into the Olympics? With the increase in esports competitions globally, one would assume that it is only a matter of time before these global competitions end up in the Olympics. One strong indicator that this may come to fruition is the inclusion of esports into the Asian Games in 2018, a multisport event on a four-year schedule, similar to the Olympics. In addition, we are seeing a surge of interest in esports by streaming companies. In fact, Amazon, one of the world's largest companies, owns Twitch, a well-known streaming service for gamers. It is likely that Amazon's biggest competitors will soon follow suit.[5]

In an article on the website Venturebeat, David Hoppe compares the esports industry and NASA. "Esports in the last two decades has become a billion-dollar industry on a trajectory that would make NASA jealous. Players are celebrities, tournaments fill arenas with screaming fans, and sponsors are increasingly injecting real money into the esports ecosystem."[6] It is only logical to mindfully consider where much of that financial support derives from. In most cases, it is straight from the industry itself. With a large percentage of the investments coming from those who profit from its success, the esports financial world is cyclical. Consideration must be given to how esports protects that fragile ecosystem. With topics like potential athlete unions, cheating scandals (especially as betting on esports grows exponentially), and the lure of college scholarships, esports as a whole must ensure that the avenues become roads of upstanding positivity and not fall victim to negative influences. It is uncharted territory for esports. However, we can look to the pitfalls that traditional sports have encountered for years, to learn from them and do better.

Regardless of the challenges that lie ahead, esports has a big and bright future. With a growing population of participants, new games, and competitions emerging regularly, and the interest and growing support of society, esports is quickly becoming an integral part of our world. That said, and while it is important to take into consideration everything that will impact its existence, we should also focus on what esports represents to the individual student. The concept of being included in something that is bigger than yourself, the camaraderie of belonging to a team, the pride of celebrating victory, and admiration from a school community are all rewards that every educator strives to provide for students, regardless of the paths they follow.

AN ESPORTS PARTNER FOR K–12 EDUCATION

Getting started with any new program can feel like a daunting challenge, and even more so when you feel isolated and without a support system. Fortunately for educators, NASEF has been leading the way for K–12 educators and helping spread the passion of providing competitive gameplay and esports learning experiences with educators and students as their mission.

We want to welcome Gerald Solomon, executive director of the Samueli Foundation and founder of NASEF, and Laylah Bulman, program officer for the Samueli Foundation and executive director of the Florida Scholastic Esports League (FLSEL) to share a bit about the types of programs, curricula, and support available through NASEF. What follows in this appendix comes from them.

Esports provides a fantastic environment for connecting play and learning. For example, participating in a scholastic esports program such as NASEF offers all the benefits of the esports experience that, when paired with state-approved curricula, puts fun back into learning. Many organizations run tournaments for high schoolers, but lasting education demands an intentional framework, and one that is evidence based and department of education approved. By tapping into students' love of esports and related components of the ecosystem, it is possible to genuinely engage youth in the meaningful learning of life and career skills. Scholastic esports, not just esports, is the key.

NASEF has developed an evidence- and research-based program that incorporates state education standards into league play of popular video games while maintaining an authentic gamers' experience. Similarly, esports-centric classes impart time-tested principles with illustrations from the games, community, and the ecosystem to make the lessons fun and memorable.

Online platforms like esports are the new social gathering places for kids. NASEF believes that esports, when infused with state-credentialed curricula, can be leveraged for an even greater benefit, to help students grow their STEM interests and develop valued skills that will be needed for success in the future workforce.

NASEF's foundation is based upon several principles: First, it is a scholastic platform that uses esports as the Trojan Horse to get kids excited about learning. Second, it is free, because education is a fundamental right. And lastly, it is evidence- and research-based, assessing the nexus between the curriculum and the play of esports.

"Millions of teenagers are playing esports, leading many parents and educators to wonder how to infuse positive elements into the outrageously popular video game community and culture," said Dr. Constance Steinkuehler, professor of informatics at UCI and NASEF's education and research lead. "NASEF provides schools with the tools they need to give teens a complete experience that combines the fun of gaming with deeply embedded education on relevant real-world skills."

HOW NASEF'S EDUCATION PERMEATES ESPORTS

In- and Out-of-School Learning

Renowned education experts from the Orange County Department of Education, researchers from the University of California, Irvine, and UCI Esports (the 2018 College *League of Legends* National Champion) carefully examined the esports ecosystem to create what is currently the

only state-approved full four-year high school and CTE-track curriculum connecting education to esports. They were able to integrate education into esports clubs in the following ways:

- An environment was created to nurture collaboration, communication, and school pride.
- Near-peer professional coaches guide students to develop
  social-emotional skills and build a positive gaming culture, as well
  as improve their gameplay.
- Professionals lead career-focused workshops, clinics, and mentoring sessions, incorporating engineering, technology, and entrepreneurship principles.
- Students are mentored to build crucial twenty-first-century skills.
- School clubs gain access to dozens of toolkits that help members
  with important tasks, like creating a club charter and code of conduct, fundraising, and building an online presence.
- An entire state-approved curriculum for high school and CTE was
  developed that can be used as a framework for connecting learning and play in any school or out-of-school program.

Beyond the Game

High school students interested in a variety of STEM and creative careers
should have the opportunity for real-world experience in those areas.
NASEF offers recognition and mentorship opportunities in Beyond the
Game challenges in seventeen categories of competition, such as:

- Ready, Set, Draw: Create Fan Art
- Making Money Moves: Host a Fundraiser
- Let's Get Hype: Create a Club or Team Video
- Adopt a Bot: Upgrade Your Discord Server
- Surf's Up: Design Your Club Website[1]

Aaron Teats, vice-president and CMO of the Anaheim Ducks NHL
team, said, "In every sport, for every professional player, hundreds or even
thousands of professionals work to support the gameplay in marketing,

content creation, data analysis, communications, and more. These challenges bring high school scholastic esports clubs the same reality that exists in the professional sports world. NASEF's work to help students prepare for the real world is impressive."

Classroom Opportunities for Learning

The rapidly growing esports video game ecosystem provides a unique wealth of material for education around mythology, plot, and character, as well as business-centric principles, such as critical thinking, ethics, persuasive writing, collaboration, and developing and making professional presentations. Video game programs are most effective when properly designed and implemented by credentialed educators and when approved by state curriculum decision-makers.

We shouldn't be afraid to leverage esports for learning just because it is a sport or, for some, just as a business venture. The ability to go to where the students are and capture their attention offers a rare opportunity. The combined enthusiasm of students and teachers for play and classroom study tells us we are onto something big. We have introduced a disruptive and innovative way to reengage kids in education.

English Language Arts (ELA) Platform

NASEF's ELA Integrated Courses for grades nine to twelve were designed by a team of professors and researchers. The courses are California approved for "B" designation, which means they meet graduation requirements as core classes, not electives—an important distinction. They are open sourced and modifiable for state-specific standards throughout the country.

Direct connections are made between esports and content standards (NGSS, ISTE, SEL, CTE, and Common Core).

Courses include:

- English 9 + Game Design[2]
- English 10 + Entrepreneurship[3]
- English 11 + Marketing[4]
- English 12 + Organizers[5]

Career Technical Education

Following state approval of the high school ELA curriculum, these same educators designed a CTE state-approved curriculum, which is also available free to all schools and students. It sets forth a multiyear sequence of courses for students in grades eight to twelve that integrate core academic and technical knowledge with twenty-five courses. The curriculum is designed around the four major esports sectors:

- Strategists
- Organizers
- Content creators
- Entrepreneurs

The curriculum will provide pathways to fifteen careers, including but not limited to:

- Event Planner
- Analyst
- Fandom art
- Marketing
- Theory crafter
- Shoutcaster
- Streamer
- Journalist
- Web developer

Middle School Courses

Because esports offers such an innovative and unique experiential opportunity for learning, middle school administrators and teachers asked NASEF to extend its curriculum to the middle school platform. NASEF complied, and now offers a field-tested curriculum for middle school students as well. As with the high school and CTE curriculum, it integrates standards-based academic and technical knowledge in esports.

NASEF Affiliate Component: GSE & FLSEL

As NASEF expanded, it decided to utilize the proven federated model used by many youth organizations like YWCA, YMCA, Boys & Girls Clubsof America, and other out-of-school programs, providing global oversight and programming while allowing local autonomy and control, and scalability. Laylah Bulman, an educator and professional from Florida, stepped up and decided to create the first NASEF affiliate, the Florida Scholastic Esports League (FLSEL).[6] In six short months, Bulman took the NASEF model to new heights, enlisting eleven school districts and over a thousand students.

Shortly thereafter, Steve and Chris started Garden State Esports (GSE)[7], the New Jersey NASEF affiliate that looks to not only provide onboarding and support for New Jersey schools interested in esports, but also acts as a governing body for esports in New Jersey. Garden State Esports is also unique in having incorporated their nationwide middle school *Rocket League* coalition into Garden State Esports. The vertical move of organizing all schools interested in esports in New Jersey but also the horizontal move of running a middle school esports league that anyone in the country can join, is a unique take on running an affiliate.

Most importantly, FLSEL and GSE created an updated model whereby gaming and esports serve as the centerpiece of the experience surrounded by student-led and -developed activities that showcase all of the domains. Thus when parents, educators and others observe the scholastic esports competition, they also observe student contests and work around such activities as logo design, social media activities, event management, business plan development, fandom art, data analytics, and other STEAM skills and attributes essential to the future-ready workforce. FLSEL and GSE embrace the mission that NASEF is far more than simply competition and gaming. It is a true model of the "scholastic" approach to using esports as a Trojan horse to engage students where they are, connecting their passion with purpose, education, and career development that can last a lifetime. Other states and countries have since come on as NASEF affiliate organizations as well.

Lasting Impact

Researchers at the University of California, Irvine, secured Institutional Review Board (IRB) approval to study NASEF's curriculum in esports and found students improved in nearly every outcome variable measured, including STEM career interest, school engagement, relationships with both peers and adults, critical thinking, and many others. Gerald Solomon, NASEF's executive director, sums it up well: "Teens love esports—the games, the camaraderie, and an entire ecosystem that includes shoutcasting, digital art, fan fiction, and yes, tournaments. We've developed NASEF to foster development of real-world skills through that ecosystem."[8]

Encouraging Positive Behaviors and Diversity

In order to provide an environment to help students learn, grow, and thrive, scholastic-based esports clubs and teams require a code of conduct. Diversity doesn't just happen—to achieve it requires intentionality. NASEF has developed code of conduct document that serves as the foundation for participation. All clubs review, personalize, and adopt it. All are expected to adhere to the same standard: to ensure that the esports environment is inclusive, supportive, and respectful.

Esports are for everyone, and NASEF stands with AnyKey in asking students to commit to a high standard of personal character and behavior, rising above the negativity, toxic behavior, and discrimination that exist in many gaming communities. NASEF and AnyKey are focused on creating a gaming ecosystem that welcomes everyone and includes all, no matter their shape, size, color, gender, background, disability, or beliefs.

AnyKey is intent on transforming esports into a better place for all, and NASEF has partnered with them for that mission. Therefore all students participating are expected to adhere to a formalized code of conduct.

GLOSSARY OF COMMON ESPORTS TERMS

Bad manners (BM): Someone who is being rude and disrespectful.

Bugs: Errors in a video game.

Buff: Any change to the game that makes a character or strategy stronger.

Build: A player choosing the skills, abilities, or loadout of their character—literally how a player "builds" their character.

Carry: A player carries their team when they are so much better than their teammates that they can be wholly responsible for victory.

Cheese: A specific strategy that is powerful yet requires little skill to execute. Often leads to anger on the side of the player being cheesed.

Composition (Comp): The makeup of an esports team that has characters that fill roles. For example, the comp of a team may be two DPS, two healers, or two tanks.

Cross-platform play: The ability to play across game environments. Some games can only be played competitively on the same gaming platform (e.g., players on an Xbox can only play against other players on Xbox, or players on a computer cannot play against players on a console). Cross-platform is becoming increasingly common.

Cut scene: Noninteractive part of a videogame used to give exposition in a story. Usually found in role-playing games.

Damage per second (DPS): The calculation of how much damage a character or ability does over time.

Downloadable content (DLC): Add-ons and extra content that can be purchased to enhance the gameplay experience for existing games.

Emote: An action a character can perform that is usually accompanied by sound and animation to convey emotion and communicate with other players.

Esports: Competitive digital gaming. Referred to properly as *esports*, not *eSports* or *Esports*. Capitalized as a proper noun or first word of a sentence.

Farming: Also known as *grinding*, the process of doing the same thing over and over again in a game in search of a specific item or to gain a certain amount of experience points to level up.

Fighting games: Typically involve one-on-one gameplay in which each player chooses a character with special abilities to battle it out in a virtual arena. Popular competitive fighting games include *Super Smash Bros.*, *Street Fighter*, and *Tekken*.

First-person shooter (FPS): Games displayed from the player's perspective, typically showing the player's arms holding the weapon or items they are currently using. Popular FPS games include *Overwatch*, *CS: GO*, and *Call of Duty*.

Free to play (F2P): Games that can be played without a fee. Many allow microtransactions.

Good game (GG): Usually typed at the end of an esports match by the losing player, signifying that they have given up. Considered rude if the winning player types it before the losing player.

Good luck have fun (GLHF): Commonly typed at the beginning of matches, like a virtual handshake.

Griefing: The purposeful harassment of one player by another. Griefers want to make others angry and ruin the fun.

Healer: Player position characterized by a character class that has the ability to heal teammates. Healers typically play back and support the offensive players.

Keyboard warrior: A person who makes abusive or aggressive posts on the internet, concealing their true identity.

Loot box: Packages of in-game rewards containing coveted items or skins for players. sometimes free, sometimes available for a fee (microtransaction).

Meta (also meta game):The best way to play the game, usually made up of the tactics, characters, and skills that are most likely to lead to victory. Players not following the meta are playing "off meta." After a patch or change to the game, the meta may shift.

Microtransactions: The ability to purchase in-game, usually aesthetic items, which modify the appearance of a character, but some impact the game play (see *pay to win*).

Massively multiplayer online (MMO): Games played by large groups of people online at a one time. Popular MMORPGs (massively multiplayer online role-playing games) include *EverQuest*, *World of Warcraft*, and *Final Fantasy XIV*.

Multiplayer online battle arena (MOBA): Games that show a top-down view of the playing area. Players typically control a hero that levels up through the game and earns abilities based on level and resources accumulated. Popular MOBAs include *League of Legends*, *Dota 2*, and *Heroes of the Storm*.

Nerf: Any change to the game that makes a character or strategy weaker, named after the foam children's toys.

Non-player character (NPC): a character in the game that is not controlled by a player, often refers to a character you will interact with in the game that will guide you through the story. Generally not hostile toward the player.

Online collectible card game / collectible card games (CCGs): games in which players form decks based on the cards they own. Cards typically have abilities, and players battle it out by playing offensive and defensive cards. In most CCGs, players can purchase decks or cards to improve their strategy. Online CCGs are digital versions of games like Magic: The Gathering and Pokémon Trading Card Game and include *Hearthstone* and *Magic: The Gathering Arena*.

Overpowered (OP): Anything considered to be so powerful that it is unfair or broken. Whether something is OP or not is always a debate in the esports world.

Patch: Incremental changes made to a video game by the developer that fix bugs and/or buffs and nerfs strategies, characters, or abilities.

Pay to win (PTW): Games with in-game microtransactions that impact the gameplay, giving a player who is willing to pay for items with real money a distinct advantage.

Player versus player (PVP): Human players playing against one another. Many games have player-versus-player or player-versus-environment (PVE) modes. Competitive gaming tends to focus on PVP, but competitive gameplay, including speed runs and other game types may not involve PVP.

Racing games: A genre of games (car, motorcycle, etc.). *Gran Turismo*, *iRacing*, and *Forza* are among the popular titles. During the COVID-19 suspension of professional sports, the NASCAR *iRacing* invitational featuring pro drivers in a virtual event was the most watched esports TV show to date.[1]

Rage quit: To become so angry that you quit the game in the middle of a match.

Real-time strategy (RTS): a genre of game that is shown from a top-down view and involves the player gathering resources, constructing buildings, generating and upgrading units, and sending armies into battle against other players. Popular competitive RTS games include *StarCraft*, *StarCraft II*, and *Warcraft III*.

Salty: The negative attitude of a frustrated player. A sore loser.

Shoutcasting: Broadcasting esports events, essentially the sportscasters and commentators of competitive gaming.

Skins: The cosmetics of a character. Using skins, you can customize how characters look or act.

Sports games: Traditional sports translated into video games. Football, soccer, basketball, hockey, baseball, tennis, and others have been played competitively for years. Popular sports games include a number of franchises, including *Madden*, *NBA 2K*, *FIFA*, and *Rocket League*. When sports were suspended due to COVID-19, many esports competitions were televised, often including professional players playing digital versions of their sport.

Streamer: Someone who broadcasts gaming events or matches to a live audience. Popular streaming platforms include Twitch, Mixer, and YouTube

Support: A support character's role is to heal, buff, and/or provide utility. They boost the overall performance of their team by increasing their survival, speed, and/or damage output. Supports are generally not very good duelists and are best surrounded by teammates.

Tank: A player position characterized by strength and durability. Typically plays up front to deal and take damage.

Tilt: A player who begins playing poorly out of anger or frustration, behavior that often impacts the entire team. The term originates from pinball, where a player would bang the machine out of anger or frustration, often losing their turn as a result.

Toxic: Poor behavior and negative attitude (toxicity) toward other players. The equivalent of bad sportsmanship. Often creates an unsafe online gaming experience for others.

Triggered: Becoming angry at the actions of griefers, trolls, or the events in-game. Being triggered can lead to playing tilted.

Trolling: The purposeful harassment of one player by another. Trolls want to make others angry and ruin the fun.

Video on demand (VOD): replays of matches that can be reviewed and analyzed as part of coaching and strategy development.

Introduction

1 Derrick Bryson Taylor and Niraj Choski, "This *Fortnite* World Cup Winner Is 16 and $3 Million Richer," *New York Times,* July 29, 2019.

2 Esports Charts, "Worlds 2018—200 Million Viewers at Once," https://escharts.com/blog/worlds-2018-final; Patrick Dorsey, "'*League of Legends*' Ratings Top NBA finals, World Series Clinchers," *ESPN,* December 1, 2014, https://www.espn.com/espn/story/_/page/instantawesome-leagueoflegends-141201/league-legends-championships-watched-more-people-nba-finals-world-series-clinchers.

3 Kevin Webb, "More Than 100 million People Watched the '*League of Legends*' World Championship, Cementing Its Place as the Most Popular Esport," *Business Insider*, December 18, 2019, https://www.businessinsider.com/league-of-legends-world-championship-100-million-viewers-2019-12.

4 Lucy Handley, "Super Bowl Draws Lowest TV Audience in More Than a Decade, Early Data Show," CNBC, February 5, 2019, https://www.cnbc.com/2019/02/05/super-bowl-draws-lowest-tv-audience-in-more-than-a-decade-nielsen.html.

5 "With Viewership and Revenue Booming, Esports Set to Compete with Traditional Sports," *Syracuse Online Business*, January 18, 2019, https://onlinebusiness.syr.edu/blog/esports-to-compete-with-traditional-sports.

6 Julia Alexander, "*Fortnite* Hits 125 Million Players in Less Than a Year, Says Epic Games," *Polygon*, June 12, 2018, https://www.polygon.com/2018/6/12/17456838/fortnite-125-million-players-tournament-world-cup.

7 Adam Fitch, "ESL and Big Ten Network Launch Collegiate *League of Legends* Season," *Esports Insider*, February 16, 2019, https://esportsinsider.com/2019/02/esl-big-ten-network-league-of-legends.

8   Chris Baker, "Stewart Brand Recalls First 'Spacewar' Video Game Tournament," *Rolling Stone,* May 25, 2016, https://www.rollingstone.com/culture/culture-news/stewart-brand-recalls-first-spacewar-video-game-tournament-187669/.

9   Ameen Ghazizadeh, "The Evolution of Competitive Gaming: With a Focus on '*League of Legends,*'" blog post, January 31, 2019, https://medium.com/@aghaziza/the-evolution-of-competitive-gaming-with-a-focus-on-league-of-legends-82d3aaf08ffb.

10 Colin North, "The Story Of Billy Mitchell: The Disgraced Donkey Kong Champion," *ggn00b,* July 24, 2019, https://ggn00b.com/for-noobs/the-story-of-billy-mitchell-the-disgraced-donkey-kong-champion.

11 Peter Sciretta, "Did Steve Wiebe Reclaim His Title as The King of Kong?," blog post, March 6, 2008, https://www.slashfilm.com/did-steve-wiebe-reclaim-his-title-of-the-king-of-kong.

12 Ron Caraos, "Billy Mitchell to Set the Record Straight about His Disputed 'Donkey Kong,' 'Pac-Man' Records," *Tech Times,* April 16, 2018, https://www.techtimes.com/articles/225268/20180416/billy-mitchell-to-set-the-record-straight-about-his-disputed-donkey-kong-pac-man-records.htm.

13 Jonathan H. Kantor, "Inside 'The Wizard': The Cult '80s Movie That Introduced 'Mario 3' and Predicted E-Sports," *Ranker,* February 27, 2020, https://www.ranker.com/list/the-wizard-movie-e-sports/jonathan-kantor.

14 "Why South Korea is the Home of Esports," *Game Trends,* July 23, 2019, https://gametrends.com/why-south-korea-is-the-home-of-esports.

15 Arash Markazi, "Daigo and JWong: The Legacy of Street Fighter's Moment 37," *ESPN,* August 25, 2016, https://www.espn.com/esports/story/_/id/17391663/daigo-jwong-legacy-street-fighter-moment-37.

16 Elaine Teng, "Living the Stream," *ESPN,* September 19, 2018, http://www.espn.com/espn/feature/story/_/id/24710688/fortnite-legend-ninja-living-stream.

17 Emily Rand, "Former NFL Star Ahman Green Is Becoming an Esports Coach," *ESPN,* February 18, 2020, https://www.espn.com/esports/

story/_/id/28730743/former-nfl-star-ahman-green-becoming-esports
-coach.

18 Fair Haven Innovates, "FH Knights Esports," http://www.
fairhaveninnovates.com/fhkesports.

19 Chris Aviles, "New Jersey Middle School Esports Team Is 1st of Its Kind,"
YouTube video, 2:52, June 12, 2019, https://www.youtube.com/
watch?v=sQl9kloDNIQ; "Forming the Foundation for Esports in NJ,"
PBS-NJTV News, April 2, 2019, https://www.pbs.org/video/mishkin-
e-sports-tryouts-1554214903.

Chapter One

1 CASEL, "What is SEL?," https://casel.org/what-is-sel.

2 CASEL, "SEL Impact," https://casel.org/impact.

3 CASEL, "2017 Meta-Analysis," https://casel.org/2017-meta-analysis.

4 Clive Belfield et al., "The Economic Value of Social and Emotional
Learning," https://blogs.edweek.org/edweek/rulesforengagement/
SEL-Revised.pdf.

5 Damon E. Jones, Mark Greenberg, and Max Crowley, "Early
Social-Emotional Functioning and Public Health," *AJPH*, October
9, 2015, https://ajph.aphapublications.org/doi/full/10.2105/
AJPH.2015.302630.

6 CASEL, "SEL Impact," https://casel.org/impact.

7 The Aspen Institute, "Calls for Coaches: Coaching Social and
Emotional Skills in Youth Sports," http://nationathope.org/
wp-content/uploads/callforcoaches_final_web_v2.pdf.

8 CASEL, "Approaches," https://casel.org/what-is-sel-4/approaches.

9 Vicki David, "James O'Hagan: 5 Reasons to Bring ESports to your
School," *The Cool Cat Teacher* (blog), May 11, 2018, https://www.
coolcatteacher.com/e310.

10 Corporate Finance Institute, "SMART Goal," https://
corporatefinanceinstitute.com/resources/knowledge/other/smart
-goal.

11 University of Houston, "The Privilege Walk Exercise," https://www.
    uh.edu/cdi/diversity_education/resources/activities/pdf/privilege
    -walk.pdf.

12 EverFi, Inc., "The Importance of Bystander Intervention Training:
    A Real-Life Case Study," March 2, 2020, https://everfi.com/blog/
    higher-education/the-importance-of-bystander-intervention
    -a-real-life-case-study.

13 National Sleep Foundation, "Facts and Stats," October 23,
    2019, https://drowsydriving.org/about/facts-and-stats.

14 Medline Plus, "Benefits of Exercise," October 4, 2019, https://
    medlineplus.gov/benefitsofexercise.html.

15 Coleman Hamstead, "Adderall Presents Esports with an Enigma,"
    Washington Post, February 13, 2020, https://www.washingtonpost.
    com/video-games/esports/2020/02/13/esports-adderall-drugs.

16 Conor Heffernan, "Drug-Taking in Ancient Times," *Physical Culture
    Study,* November 13, 2014, https://physicalculturestudy.com/2014/
    11/13/drug-taking-in-ancient-times.

17 Michele J. Moore and Chudley E. Werch, "Sport and Physical Activity
    Participation and Substance Use Among Adolescents," *Journal
    of Adolescent Health* 36, No. 6 (June 2005), 486–93, https://www.
    sciencedirect.com/science/article/abs/pii/S1054139X04002605.

18 Coleman Hamstead, "Adderall Presents Esports with an Enigma,"
    Washington Post, February 13, 2020, https://www.washingtonpost
    .com/video-games/esports/2020/02/13/esports-adderall-drugs.

19 Alex Hutchinson, "Can Mindfulness Training Make You a Better
    Athlete?," *Outside,* September 15, 2015, https://www.outsideonline
    .com/2016861/can-mindfulness-training-make-you-better-athlete.

20 Luke Winkie, "Retired At 20: A Pro Gamer's Life after Esports," *Kotaku*
    (blog), December 8, 2015, https://kotaku.com/retired-at-20-a-pro
    -gamer-s-life-after-esports-1746907605.

21 Suzanne Degges-White, "3 Signs of Burnout and 15 Ways to
    Reduce It," *Psychology Today,* October 23, 2019, https://www.
    psychologytoday.com/us/blog/lifetime-connections/201910/3-signs
    -burnout-and-15-ways-reduce-it.

22 Luke Kerr-Dineen, "Here Are Your Odds of Becoming a Professional Athlete (They're Not Good)," *For the Win* (blog), July 27, 2016, https://ftw.usatoday.com/2016/07/here-are-your-odds-of-becoming-a-professional-athlete-theyre-not-good; Tony Manfred, "Here Are the Odds That Your Kid Becomes a Professional Athlete (Hint: They're Small)," *Business Insider*, February 10, 2012, https://www.businessinsider.com/odds-college-athletes-become-professionals-2012-2; Josh K. Elliott, "The 0.1 Per Cent: How Esports Pros Make a Career Playing Video Games," *Global News*, September 2, 2018, https://globalnews.ca/news/4420706/esports-starcraft-lol-pro-gamer-dota; Dan Starkey, "Your Odds of Being an eAthlete," *Kotaku* (blog), August 12, 2014, https://kotaku.com/your-odds-of-being-an-eathlete-esports-is-rapidly-becom-1620528958.

23 Matt Hanson, "What It Takes to Become a Professional Esports Player," *Tech Radar*, October 3, 2019, https://www.techradar.com/news/what-it-takes-to-become-a-professional-esports-player; Alex Hern, "Why My Dream of Becoming a Pro Gamer Ended in Utter Failure," January 28, 2016, https://www.theguardian.com/technology/2016/jan/28/my-dream-to-become-pro-gamer-ended-in-utter-failure.

24 Ronnie Young, "A Culture of Rage in Competitive Gaming," *Medium* (blog), July 9, 2016, https://medium.com/@Endless_Dystopia/a-culture-of-rage-in-competitive-gaming-ec66c7dff97e.

25 Alysha Tsuji, "Teammates Had to Be Tossed from a Soccer Game After Fighting Against Each Other," *For the Win* (blog), December 3, 2016, https://ftw.usatoday.com/2016/12/soccer-teammates-red-cards-tossed-ejected-fight-each-other.

26 Howard Berkes, "Nazi Olympics Tangled Politics and Sport," *NPR*, June 7, 2008, https://www.npr.org/templates/story/story.php?storyId=91246674; United States Holocaust Memorial Museum, "Indoctrinating Youth," https://encyclopedia.ushmm.org/content/en/article/indoctrinating-youth; Karim Zidan, "Fascist Fight Clubs: How White Nationalists Use MMA as a Recruiting Tool," *The Guardian*, September 11, 2018, https://www.theguardian.com/sport/2018/

sep/11/far-right-fight-clubs-mma-white-nationalists; Markus Deggerich and Maximillian Popp, "Neo-Nazis Seek New Blood among Cage Fighters," *Der Spiegel International*, December 4, 2013, https://www.spiegel.de/international/germany/german-neo-nazis-use-violent-free-fighting-sport-to-recruit-a-893742.html.

27 Caitlin Gibson, "'Do You Have White Teenage Sons? Listen Up.' How White Supremacists Are Recruiting Boys Online," *Washington Post*, September 17, 2019, https://www.washingtonpost.com/lifestyle/on-parenting/do-you-have-white-teenage-sons-listen-up-how-white-supremacists-are-recruiting-boys-online/2019/09/17/f081e806-d3d5-11e9-9343-40db57cf6abd_story.html.

28 Dan Murphy, "Army Football Program Dropped Motto of White Supremacist Origin," *ESPN*, December 5, 2019, https://www.espn.com/college-football/story/_/id/28232249/army-football-program-dropped-motto-white-supremacist-origin.

29 Arijeta Lajka, "Esports Players Burn Out Young as the Grind Takes Mental, Physical Toll," *CBS News*, December 21, 2018, https://www.cbsnews.com/news/esports-burnout-in-video-gaming-cbsn-originals.

30 Micah Shippee, *WanderlustEDU* (San Diego: Dave Burgess Consulting, Inc., 2019).

Chapter Two

1 Chris Burns, "Decade-Long Study Shows Video Games Not Linked to Negative Social Behavior," *Slash Gear* (blog), November 18, 2013, https://www.slashgear.com/decade-long-study-shows-video-games-not-linked-to-negative-social-behavior-18305824.

2 Andrew W. Przybylski and Netta Weinstein, *Royal Society Open Science* 6, no. 2 (February 2019), https://royalsocietypublishing.org/doi/10.1098/rsos.171474.

3 Ollie Barder, "New Study Shows That There Is No Link Between Violent Video Games and Aggression in Teenagers," *Forbes*, February 15, 2019, https://www.forbes.com/sites/olliebarder/2019/02/15/new

-study-shows-that-there-is-no-link-between-violent-video-games-and
-aggression-in-teenagers.

4   University of Oxford, "Violent Video Games Found Not to Be
    Associated with Adolescent Aggression," February 13, 2019, https://
    www.ox.ac.uk/news/2019-02-13-violent-video-games-found-not-be
    -associated-adolescent-aggression.

5   American Psychological Association, "Resolution on Violent Video
    Games," https://www.apa.org/about/policy/resolution-violent-video
    -games.pdf.

6   American Psychological Association, "APA Reaffirms Position on
    Violent Video Games and Violent Behavior," March 3, 2020, https://
    www.apa.org/news/press/releases/2020/03/violent-video-games
    -behavior.

7   Kate McKenna, "Social Media, but Not Video Games, Linked to
    Depression in Teens, According to Montreal Study," *CBC News*, July
    15, 2019, https://www.cbc.ca/news/canada/montreal/social-media
    -mental-health-screen-time-instagram-facebook-video-games
    -study-1.5211782.

8   Ollie Barder, "New Study Shows That There Is No Link Between Violent
    Video Games and Aggression in Teenagers," *Forbes*, February 15,
    2019, https://www.forbes.com/sites/olliebarder/2019/02/15/new
    -study-shows-that-there-is-no-link-between-violent-video-games-and
    -aggression-in-teenagers.

9   Emily VanDerWerff, "#Gamergate: Here's Why Everybody in the
    Video Game World is Fighting," *Vox*, October 13, 2014, https://www.
    vox.com/2014/9/6/6111065/gamergate-explained-everybody
    -fighting.

10 Joe Simone, "Solidifying a Place for Esports in the Classroom,"
    EdTech, March 19, 2020, https://edtechmagazine.com/K–12/
    article/2020/03/solidifying-place-esports-classroom.

11 Martin Schutz, "Science Shows That Esports Professionals Are Real
    Athletes," *DW*, December 3, 2016, https://www.dw.com/en/science
    -shows-that-esports-professionals-are-real-athletes/a-19084993.

12 Jordan Cook, "PlayVS, Bringing Esports Infrastructure to High Schools, Picks Up $15 Million," *Tech Crunch*, June 4, 2018, https://techcrunch. com/2018/06/04/playvs-bringing-esports-infrastructure-to-high-scho ols-picks-up-15-million.

13 H. B. Duran, "Celebrating Women in Esports, Part 2: Increasing Engagement," *The Esports Observer*, March 8, 2019, https:// esportsobserver.com/women-in-esports-part-2.

14 Rebekah Valentine, "Esports' Urgent Need for Visible Gender Diversity," *gamesindustry.biz* (blog), December 20, 2018, https://www. gamesindustry.biz/articles/2018-12-20-esports-urgent-need-for-visible -gender-diversity.

15 H. B. Duran, "Celebrating Women in Esports, Part 2: Increasing Engagement," *The Esports Observer*, March 8, 2019, https:// esportsobserver.com/women-in-esports-part-2.

16 H. B. Duran, "Celebrating Women in Esports, Part 2: Increasing Engagement," *The Esports Observer*, March 8, 2019, https:// esportsobserver.com/women-in-esports-part-2.

17 Ben Johnson, "Esports, Gaming Diversity Discussed at Inclusive Sports Summit," *CU Independent*, March 2, 2020, https://cuindependent .com/2020/03/02/esports-inclusive-sports-summit.

18 Se Jin Kim, "Gender Inequality in eSports Participation: Examining *League of Legends*" (Master's thesis, University of Texas at Austin, 2017), https://repositories.lib.utexas.edu/bitstream/ handle/2152/62914/KIM-THESIS-2017.pdf?sequence=1&isAllowed=y.

19 "Mischief League," https://www.mischiefleague.org/, accessed May 6, 2020.

20 Jason Krell, "Diversity, Inclusion Remain a Problem in Esports Industry," *Global Sport Matters* (blog), October 18, 2019, https:// globalsportmatters.com/culture/2019/10/18/diversity-inclusion -remain-a-problem-in-esports-industry.

21 Victoria Rideout, Alexis Lauricella, and Ellen Wartella, "Children, Media, and Race: Media Use among White, Black, Hispanic, and Asian American Children." Report for the Center on Media and Human Development, School of Communication, Northwestern

University, June 2011, http://cmhd.northwestern.edu/wp-content/
uploads/2011/06/SOCconfReportSingleFinal-1.pdf.

22 Nielsen, "How Diverse Are Video Gamers—And the Characters
They Play?," March 24, 2015, https://www.nielsen.com/us/
en/insights/article/2015/how-diverse-are-video-gamers-an
d-the-characters-they-play.

23 Morgan Romine, "12 Best Practices for Diversity and Inclusion in
Collegiate Esports," *Medium* (blog), October 11, 2019, https://
medium.com/@rhoulette/12-best-practices-for-diversity-and-inclusion
-in-collegiate-esports-d15d3efc8b9a.

Chapter Three

1 Rich Huggan, "Esports Is Hiring—And You Don't Need to Be a Player,"
VentureBeat (blog), August 30, 2018, https://venturebeat.com/2018/
08/30/esports-is-hiring-and-you-dont-need-to-be-a-player.

Chapter Four

1 NASEF, "Curriculum," https://www.esportsfed.org/learning/curriculum.

2 Kristy Custer and Michael Russell, "Gaming Concepts," https://static1.
squarespace.com/static/5317bce9e4b06ab557245f78/t/
5d10f8d4bedffa00014e1252/1561393400257/Gaming+Concepts.pdf.

3 Microsoft Education Center, "Build a School to Career Pipeline with
Esports and Gaming Concepts," https://education.microsoft.com/
en-us/course/d40087b3/overview.

4 ESRB, "Ratings Guide," https://www.esrb.org/ratings-guide.

5 Mike Sullivan, "High Schools Launch Indiana's First Interscholastic
Esports League," *Fox 59*, September 25, 2019, https://fox59.com/
news/high-schools-launch-indianas-first-interscholastic-esports
-league.

6 A few months after writing the GOATS example above, Blizzard,
the creators of *Overwatch*, totally changed the rules of the game.
Overwatch now locks players into the older 2-2-2 meta meaning

GOATS is now impossible to play. They made this change because GOATS was boring for fans to watch. While the example of GOATS is still valid, let this serve as a reminder that at any time a game company can completely change the way the game is played!

7   NASEF, "FAQ," https://www.esportsfed.org/about/faq.

8   NFHS, "Esports," https://www.nfhs.org/sports-resource-content/esports.

9   High School Esports League, "FAQ," https://www.highschoolesportsleague.com/partnership-faq.

10 Thomas Baker, "Will the NCAA Move to Sponsor U.S. Collegiate Esports? The Story So Far and Key Issues to Watch," *Law in Sport* (blog), March 26, 2019, https://www.lawinsport.com/topics/item/will-the-ncaa-move-to-sponsor-u-s-collegiate-esports-the-story-so-far-and-key-issues-to-watch.

11 Tespa, "What is Tespa?," https://compete.tespa.org/about.

12 EGF, "Home," http://egfederation.com/.

13 Esports for Edu, "RPG – eSports for Edu." https://www.esportsforedu.com/category/rpg/.

14 NASEF, "Esports Clubs in High School and Beyond: North America Scholastic Esports Federation Takes Free Clubs, Coaching, and Tournaments to Community Organizations, Equipping Students with Valuable Career Skills As They Game," August 29, 2018, www.nasef.org/news/press-room/esports-club-beyond/.

Conclusion

1   Scott Heinrich, "Esports Ride Crest of a Wave as Figures Rocket during COVID-19 Crisis," *The Guardian*, April 10, 2020, https://www.theguardian.com/sport/2020/apr/11/esports-ride-crest-of-a-wave-as-figures-rocket-during-covid-19-crisis.

2   TEXSEF, "Home," https://www.texsef.org/athome.

3   Chris Burt and Steve Isaacs, "5 Tips for Leveraging Student Interest in *Minecraft*," *District Administration* (blog), April 13, 2020, https://districtadministration.com/5-tips-for-leveraging-student-interest-through-minecraft.

4 NASEF, "Face-Off," https://www.esportsfed.org/learning/face-off.

5 J. L. Seto, "Our Predictions for the Future of Esports," *Sportscasting* (blog), April 7, 2020, https://www.sportscasting.com/our-predictions -for-the-future-of-esports.

6 David B. Hoppe, "The Future of Esports Is Bigger, Messier, and Worldwide," *VentureBeat* (blog), January 18, 2020, https:// venturebeat.com/2020/01/18/the-future-of-esports-is-bigger-messier -and-worldwide/.

Appendix

1 NASEF, "BTF Challenges," https://www.nasef.org/clubs/btg -challenges.

2 NASEF, "Grade 9," https://www.esportsfed.org/learning/curriculum/ ela/grade9.

3 NASEF, "Grade 10," https://www.esportsfed.org/learning/curriculum/ ela/grade10.

4 NASEF, "Grade 11," https://www.esportsfed.org/learning/curriculum/ ela/grade11.

5 NASEF, "Grade 12," https://www.esportsfed.org/learning/curriculum/ ela/grade12.

6 Florida Scholastic Esports League, "Home," https://flsel.org.

7 Garden State Esports League, "Home," http://gsesports.org.

8 NASEF, "Esports Clubs in High School and Beyond," https://www .esportsfed.org/news/press-room/esports-club-beyond.

Glossary

1 Jon Fingas, "NASCAR's Virtual Race Was the Most-Watched Esports TV Show to Date," *Engadget* (blog), March 25, 2020, https://www .engadget.com/2020-03-25-nascar-esports-racing-series-sets-tv -record.html.

ACKNOWLEDGMENTS

This book would not have been possible without the support and encouragement of the incredible team at Dave Burgess Consulting, Inc. including Dave and Shelley Burgess, Tara Martin, and Wendy Van Dyk. We were also fortunate enough to work again with the talented team at the Reading List, including Sal Borriello, Lindsey Alexander, Olson Pook, and Kaelin Alexander, who helped us construct a narrative and consistent flow out of the millions of ideas we had. Our gifted cover designer, Liz Schreiter, was able to take a concept we were struggling to describe and render it perfectly on the first try. Our good friend and illustrator Manuel S. Herrera showed us yet again how talented he is at creating images that perfectly capture the spirit of our ideas.

Special thanks to the trailblazers of NASEF for their support, commitment to excellence, and guidance as we stand on their shoulders. Extra special thanks to Jorrel Batac, Gerald Solomon, Laylah Bulman, Michelle Freeman, Kevin Brown, Mark Deppe, Sam Anton, Jessamyn Acebes, and NASEF scholastic Fellows Miles Harvey, JD Williams, Angelique Gianas, James Wood, and Tyler Hahn. We would like to express our gratitude to Erik Leitner and Cathy Cheo-Isaacs, who worked tirelessly alongside the NASEF team to create opportunities for students around the world to connect, create, and automate with *Minecraft* during the COVID-19 pandemic.

We are grateful for the friendship and support of our friends at ByteSpeed, including Anna Hanson, Grant Hagen, and Josh Knutson, who continue to help schools push the envelope in terms of what is possible through technology. Their learning-first focus on technology is a model that other companies should strive to emulate.

This book would not have been possible without all of the members of the education and esports communities who shared their valuable time to speak with us and contribute their thoughts and insights. Thank you to Layla Abbott, Samantha Anton, Kevin Brown, Brock Cheung, Yunhee Chi, Kimberly Lane Clark, Larry Cocco, J. Collins, Jarrett Early, Ahman Green, Bradford Harris, Dr. Chris "Doc" Haskell, Mimi Ito, Kiera Karl, Reeran Kim, Dennis Large, Carrie Linden, D. J. Moreau, James O'Hagan, Eduardo Rivera, Glenn Robbins, Katie Salen Tekinbaş, Justin Satter, Jonathan Spike, Daniel Velasquez, Chris "Topher Jaims" Vocelka, and Mike Washburn.

We would like to thank the Garden State Esports team: Dr. Matt Strobel, Phillip Strobel, Esteban Mena, Regina Schaffer, and Chris Boehmer. Thanks also go out to the wonderful staff and students of the Fair Haven school district, especially Sean McNeil, Amy Romano, Cheryl Romano, the Fair Haven Board of Education, and the FH Knights players and parents for their continued support.

Lastly, we want to extend a thank you to our Ready Learner One family, who contributed their time and insights to the development of *The Esports Education Playbook*: Dr. Micah Shippee, Craig Besnoy, Bobby Carlton, Faye Ellis, Amanda Fox, Matt Gottilla, Kenneth Shelton, Sean Williams, and Dr. Brian Chinni.

ABOUT THE AUTHORS

CHRIS AVILES

Chris Aviles is a teacher at Knollwood Middle School in Fair Haven, New Jersey. There he runs the renowned Fair Haven Innovates program he created in 2015. Part of his FH Innovates program includes the FH Knights, the first middle school esports team in the country. As coach of the FH Knights, Chris and his players take on all comers from around the country, including other middle schools, high schools, and even colleges. Chris has been involved in esports since 1998 and is passionate about growing the #esportsedu movement. Chris is a NASEF fellow and founder of Garden State Esports, a nonprofit providing guidance and resources to help schools start esports in their district. Chris still games competitively.

STEVE ISAACS

Steve Isaacs has been teaching since 1992. He developed an internationally recognized middle and high school game-development program. Steve is a champion for student choice and student voice, providing a choice-based environment to help students find and nurture their passion for learning. Steve is an educational technology influencer, community builder, and leader in game-based learning. He is actively involved in building the K–12m–to–college esports pipeline and cofounded the #esportsedu community, as well as Garden State Esports, the New Jersey affiliate of NASEF. Steve was honored as the 2016 ISTE Outstanding Teacher and the PBS Digital Innovator representing the state of New Jersey.

CHRISTINE LION-BAILEY

Christine Lion-Bailey is the chief strategy officer and cofounder of Ready Learner One LLC. She is a Google Certified Innovator and an adjunct professor of instructional technology at Ramapo College of New Jersey. Christine serves on the advisory board for the Transformative Leadership Program at Pace University's Lubin School of Business. With seventeen years of experience in education, Christine serves as an elementary principal and director of technology and innovation for the Morris Plains School District in New Jersey. She is the coauthor of *Reality Bytes: Innovative Learning Using Augmented and Virtual Reality* and cohost of the *Ready Learner One Lounge*, a virtual reality show focused on innovative solutions in teaching, learning, and training.

JESSE LUBINSKY

Jesse Lubinsky is chief learning officer of Ready Learner One LLC. He is a Google Certified Innovator and Trainer, a CoSN Certified Education Technology Leader, an adjunct professor of education technology at Pace University, a member of the Google Earth Education Experts team, and a frequent keynote speaker who has presented across North America, Europe, Asia, the Middle East, the Caribbean, and Australia. Jesse spent nearly two decades in public schools as a teacher and director of technology and innovation. He is coauthor of *Reality Bytes: Innovative Learning Using Augmented and Virtual Reality* and cohost of the *Partial Credit Podcast* and the *Ready Learner One Lounge*, a virtual reality show focused on innovations in teaching, learning, and training.

ABOUT READY LEARNER ONE

Ready Learner One LLC provides innovative solutions for learning and specializes in working with emergent technologies. Founded by passionate, experienced educators who recognize the power that technology and innovative practices have in shifting education, the Ready Learner One team offers a vast array of learning solutions. You can find out more information about us at http://readylearner.one

MORE BOOKS FROM
READY LEARNER ONE LLC

We're at the dawn of an incredible transformation in education. Augmented reality and virtual reality—technologies that were once the province of science fiction and fantasy—are faster, better, and more affordable than ever. These tools have the potential to not only inspire students, but to redefine how we teach and collaborate. But widespread adoption of AR and VR in K–12 classrooms requires taking risks, investing money and time, and training educators.

Reality Bytes makes the case for taking this leap by showing how educators are using these amazing technologies, and it provides a powerful framework to help anyone, in any school, join them. The innovative educators profiled are already designing learning experiences using AR and VR that supercharge student motivation, encourage creativity, and make otherwise impossible educational adventures accessible to all. You can do the same, using easy-to-implement resources that will revolutionize how you approach instruction. Equip your students with the skills they'll need in the future—today.

In *WanderlustEDU*, Ready Learner One CEO Dr. Micah Shippee explains how we can approach a future that is exciting but uncertain with "innovativeness," or the ability to respond creatively to the unexpected. Using relevant research and practical experience, he explores principles of self-awareness and presents practical strategies to become agents of change. Grab this book and prepare for an adventure!

MORE FROM

DAVE BURGESS
Consulting, Inc.

Since 2012, DBCI has been publishing books that inspire and equip educators to be their best. For more information on our titles or to purchase bulk orders for your school, district, or book study, visit **DaveBurgessconsulting.com/DBCIbooks**.

MORE TECHNOLOGY & TOOLS

50 Things You Can Do with Google Classroom by Alice Keeler and Libbi Miller

50 Things to Go Further with Google Classroom by Alice Keeler and Libbi Miller

140 Twitter Tips for Educators by Brad Currie, Billy Krakower, and Scott Rocco

Block Breaker by Brian Aspinall

Code Breaker by Brian Aspinall

Control Alt Achieve by Eric Curts

Google Apps for Littles by Christine Pinto and Alice Keeler

Master the Media by Julie Smith

Reality Bytes by Christine Lion-Bailey, Jesse Lubinsky, and Micah Shippee, PhD

Sail the 7 Cs with Microsoft Education by Becky Keene and Kathi Kersznowski

Shake Up Learning by Kasey Bell

Social LEADia by Jennifer Casa-Todd

Stepping Up to Google Classroom by Alice Keeler and Kimberly Mattina

Teaching Math with Google Apps by Alice Keeler and
   Diana Herrington
Teachingland by Amanda Fox and Mary Ellen Weeks

LIKE A PIRATE™ SERIES

Teach Like a PIRATE by Dave Burgess
eXPlore Like a PIRATE by Michael Matera
Learn Like a PIRATE by Paul Solarz
Play Like a PIRATE by Quinn Rollins
Run Like a PIRATE by Adam Welcome
Tech Like a PIRATE by Matt Miller

LEAD LIKE A PIRATE™ SERIES

Lead Like a PIRATE by Shelley Burgess and Beth Houf
Balance Like a PIRATE by Jessica Cabeen, Jessica Johnson, and
   Sarah Johnson
Lead beyond Your Title by Nili Bartley
Lead with Appreciation by Amber Teamann and Melinda Miller
Lead with Culture by Jay Billy
Lead with Instructional Rounds by Vicki Wilson
Lead with Literacy by Mandy Ellis

LEADERSHIP & SCHOOL CULTURE

Culturize by Jimmy Casas
Escaping the School Leader's Dunk Tank by Rebecca Coda and
   Rick Jetter
Fight Song by Kim Bearden
From Teacher to Leader by Starr Sackstein
If the Dance Floor Is Empty, Change the Song by Joe Clark
The Innovator's Mindset by George Couros
It's OK to Say "They" by Christy Whittlesey
Kids Deserve It! by Todd Nesloney and Adam Welcome

Let Them Speak by Rebecca Coda and Rick Jetter
The Limitless School by Abe Hege and Adam Dovico
Live Your Excellence by Jimmy Casas
Next-Level Teaching by Jonathan Alsheimer
The Pepper Effect by Sean Gaillard
The Principled Principal by Jeffrey Zoul and Anthony McConnell
Relentless by Hamish Brewer
The Secret Solution by Todd Whitaker, Sam Miller, and
  Ryan Donlan
Start. Right. Now. by Todd Whitaker, Jeffrey Zoul, and Jimmy Casas
Stop. Right. Now. by Jimmy Casas and Jeffrey Zoul
Teachers Deserve It by Rae Hughart and Adam Welcome
Teach Your Class Off by CJ Reynolds
They Call Me "Mr. De" by Frank DeAngelis
Thrive through the Five by Jill M. Siler
Unmapped Potential by Julie Hasson and Missy Lennard
When Kids Lead by Todd Nesloney and Adam Dovico
Word Shift by Joy Kirr
Your School Rocks by Ryan McLane and Eric Lowe

TEACHING METHODS & MATERIALS

All 4s and 5s by Andrew Sharos
Boredom Busters by Katie Powell
The Classroom Chef by John Stevens and Matt Vaudrey
The Collaborative Classroom by Trevor Muir
Copyrighteous by Diana Gill
CREATE by Bethany J. Petty
Ditch That Homework by Matt Miller and Alice Keeler
Ditch That Textbook by Matt Miller
Don't Ditch That Tech by Matt Miller, Nate Ridgway, and
  Angelia Ridgway
EDrenaline Rush by John Meehan
Educated by Design by Michael Cohen, the Tech Rabbi

The EduProtocol Field Guide by Marlena Hebern and Jon Corippo
The EduProtocol Field Guide: Book 2 by Marlena Hebern and
  Jon Corippo
Instant Relevance by Denis Sheeran
LAUNCH by John Spencer and A.insert spaceJ. Juliani
Make Learning Magical by Tisha Richmond
Pure Genius by Don Wettrick
The Revolution by Darren Ellwein and Derek McCoy
Shift This! by Joy Kirr
Skyrocket Your Teacher Coaching by Michael Cary Sonbert
Spark Learning by Ramsey Musallam
Sparks in the Dark by Travis Crowder and Todd Nesloney
Table Talk Math by John Stevens
The Wild Card by Hope and Wade King
The Writing on the Classroom Wall by Steve Wyborney

INSPIRATION, PROFESSIONAL GROWTH & PERSONAL DEVELOPMENT

Be REAL by Tara Martin
Be the One for Kids by Ryan Sheehy
The Coach ADVenture by Amy Illingworth
Creatively Productive by Lisa Johnson
Educational Eye Exam by Alicia Ray
The EduNinja Mindset by Jennifer Burdis
Empower Our Girls by Lynmara Colón and Adam Welcome
Finding Lifelines by Andrew Grieve and Andrew Sharos
The Four O'Clock Faculty by Rich Czyz
How Much Water Do We Have? by Pete and Kris Nunweiler
P Is for Pirate by Dave and Shelley Burgess
A Passion for Kindness by Tamara Letter
The Path to Serendipity by Allyson Apsey
Sanctuaries by Dan Tricarico
The SECRET SAUCE by Rich Czyz

Shattering the Perfect Teacher Myth by Aaron Hogan
Stories from Webb by Todd Nesloney
Talk to Me by Kim Bearden
Teach Better by Chad Ostrowski, Tiffany Ott, Rae Hughart, and
  Jeff Gargas
Teach Me, Teacher by Jacob Chastain
Teach, Play, Learn! by Adam Peterson
The Teachers of Oz by Herbie Raad and Nathan Lang-Raad
TeamMakers by Laura Robb and Evan Robb
Through the Lens of Serendipity by Allyson Apsey
The Zen Teacher by Dan Tricarico

CHILDREN'S BOOKS

Beyond Us by Aaron Polansky
Cannonball In by Tara Martin
Dolphins in Trees by Aaron Polansky
I Want to Be a Lot by Ashley Savage
The Princes of Serendip by Allyson Apsey
The Wild Card Kids by Hope and Wade King
Zom-Be a Design Thinker by Amanda Fox

Made in the USA
Coppell, TX
23 April 2021